POLITICAL THINKERS

edited by Professor Geraint Parry

University of Manchester

6

HOBBES

POLITICAL THINKERS

HOBBES
Morals and Politics

D. D. Raphael

Professor of Philosophy
University of London

London
George Allen & Unwin Ltd
Ruskin House   Museum Street

First published in 1977

© D. D. Raphael, 1977

ISBN 0 04 320118 0 Hardback
0 04 320119 9 Paperback

Printed in Great Britain
in 10 on 11 point Plantin
at the Alden Press, Oxford

PREFACE

Yet another book on Hobbes ? There have been so many in recent years, some of them important contributions to scholarship. This one does not claim to compete with the latter group. Although its interpretation does contain distinctive features, it has been written to meet the needs of students. Selected chapters from Hobbes's *Leviathan* can form an excellent text for elementary students either of Moral Philosophy or of Politics. Hobbes surprises, shocks, captivates, amuses, above all stimulates criticism both of himself and of our conventional wisdom. He brings up fundamental problems as much of ethics as of politics. His suggested answers make him one of the greatest of political philosophers and a highly acute, though not a deeply penetrating, thinker on ethics. While most agreeable to read, Hobbes is not always easy to understand, and the beginner needs some help. It is remarkable how few books in Moral and Political Philosophy can serve as genuine introductions for the student starting from scratch. That is the aim of this book.

It is not, however, an elementary statement of what might be found elsewhere in more elaborate form. Interpreters of Hobbes differ substantially and my view of him owes more to my own reading of his work than to what I have learned from modern scholars. The chief examples of individual interpretation are in my account of artificial obligations and rights, of the relation for Hobbes between obligation and causation, and of the continuing influence of mechanics on Hobbes's psychology and ethical theory.

The general editor of this series of Political Thinkers has particularly asked for a survey of different interpretations of the thinker concerned. In the present instance such a survey, contained in the last two chapters of the book, serves to supplement the features that I have described so far. It can guide the elementary student towards a more sophisticated approach, and at the same time it shows how far my account of Hobbes agrees with or differs from those given by other scholars.

1976   D.D.R.

CONTENTS

Chapter I

The Man

Thomas Hobbes was born at Malmesbury, in Wiltshire, on 5 April 1588. His mother gave birth to him prematurely owing to her fright at the news of the approach of the Spanish Armada. In an autobiography which he wrote in Latin verse, Hobbes says that his mother gave birth to twins, himself and fear. I mention this because there is a tradition that Hobbes was a timid man, but I am not sure that it is a reliable tradition. Hobbes showed considerable courage in publishing ideas that he knew would provoke hostility among powerful ecclesiastics and politicians. I think the tradition is founded on the following things: some of Hobbes's own remarks, such as the one I have quoted; the fact that in his philosophy he lays great stress on fear (especially the fear of death) as a motive of human behaviour; and the fact that in his old age he did not like to be left alone. Of these supposed pieces of evidence, the second, Hobbes's stress on fear as a motive, is the one most relevant to a study of his thought. Hobbes's account of human psychology has been strongly criticized; and some people have thought that he must have been describing himself and supposing that his own character was typical of mankind, when in fact it was not, because he himself was unusually timid. Now it is true that Hobbes generalizes from his own experience, and tells us at the end of the Introduction to his greatest work, *Leviathan*, that generalizations about mankind must be 'read' in oneself. Yet I doubt if Hobbes was any more subject to fear than the rest of us. Initially his psychology was an egoistic one, and this is open to criticism, as Hobbes himself must have realized because he modified it in his later work; but while one may criticize the egoism of Hobbes's *Human Nature*, it seems to me that his emphasis, in his political writings, on fear as a human motive is realistic, and that those who belittle the influence of this motive are deceiving themselves. Hobbes's account of human motives is directed towards political philosophy, and in the sphere of politics high-minded motives do not play a very large part.

Hobbes's father was a minister of religion at Malmesbury. For much of our knowledge of Hobbes's life we have to rely on the racy reminiscences of John Aubrey in *Brief Lives*. Aubrey tells us that Hobbes's father was no scholar and for his sermons simply read those of more independently minded clerics. 'A little learning went a great way with him and many other ignorant Sir Johns in those days; could only read the prayers of the Church and the homilies; and disesteemed learning . . . as not knowing the sweetness of it.' Evidently cards were more to his taste than books. On one Saturday night he had sat up late playing cards; the next day he dozed off in the middle of the service in church and must have dreamt about card-playing, since he suddenly called out loudly in his sleep, 'Clubs are trumps'. Thomas Hobbes was to remember this incident in one of his own trenchant epigrams about the relation of authority to power. In his *Dialogue . . . [on] the Common Laws of England*, Hobbes compares the exercise of political authority to playing a trump at cards – 'save that, in matter of government, when nothing else is turned up, clubs are trumps'.

After being taught by a local schoolmaster, Hobbes was sent to Oxford by a wealthy uncle. Oxford philosophers were then, as they are now, devotees of Aristotle; and there are some engaging remarks about Aristotelian philosophy (and ancient philosophy generally) in Chapter 46 of *Leviathan*:

> The natural philosophy of those schools, was rather a dream than science, and set forth in senseless and insignificant language . . . And I believe that scarce any thing can be more absurdly said in natural philosophy, than that which now is called Aristotle's *Metaphysics*; nor more repugnant to government, than much of that he hath said in his *Politics*; nor more ignorantly, than a great part of his *Ethics*.

Aubrey reports, however, that Hobbes once said to him that Aristotle's *Rhetoric* was 'rare', and this judgement I think was unfortunate. Hobbes's most serious mistakes in his psychology are simply exaggerations of what he found in Aristotle's *Rhetoric*.

On leaving Oxford Hobbes became tutor to Lord Cavendish, son of the Earl of Devonshire. With one interruption Hobbes continued to enjoy the patronage of the Cavendish family for the rest of his life. Through this connection he met a number of distinguished people, including Francis Bacon (then Lord Chancellor), Lord Herbert of Cherbury, and Ben Jonson. Francis Bacon is said to have called on Hobbes's assistance for translating some of his essays into Latin. Bacon also enjoyed conversing with Hobbes and dictating notes to him. It was Bacon's habit to dictate his thoughts to a companion as they walked, and he preferred Hobbes to any of the others, he said, because Hobbes's notes of what he had dictated made sense while those of the others did not.

Hobbes is likely to have been influenced by Bacon to some extent. In philosophy Bacon is chiefly known as the first great advocate of the inductive method in scientific inquiry, that is, the method of generalizing from observation and especially from experiments. As we shall see when I come to discuss Hobbes's method, Hobbes does not rely on induction but on deduction, that is, inferring the logical consequences of definitions. Here he is following Descartes and other mathematicians. All the great thinkers of the seventeenth century were united in their admiration for the new science and in their contempt for Aristotelian logic. Aristotelian logic is deductive, but proceeds by way of syllogisms. The new deductive logic of Descartes and others, modelled on the method of mathematics, was thought to be a different sort of thing. Now although Hobbes was evidently not impressed by Bacon's inductive method, he would have agreed warmly with Bacon's contempt for Aristotelian logic. More important, however, he agreed with Bacon's idea that 'knowledge is power'; the purpose of scientific inquiry is to acquire power over nature; inquiry is not worth the name of knowledge unless it is useful for human life.

In logical method Hobbes did not follow Bacon. His method is deductive, after the pattern of geometry. The great Rationalist philosophers of this period – Descartes, Spinoza, Leibniz – were eminently men with a talent for the mathematical style of thinking. Indeed in the case of Descartes and Leibniz it was the talent of genius. Descartes is the inventor of Analytic (or Co-ordinate) Geometry, and Leibniz shares with Newton the credit of having invented Calculus. Hobbes unfortunately did not possess any special talent for mathematics, though he thought he did. He made a fool of himself by engaging in controversy with the Professor of Mathematics at Oxford on the old problem of squaring the circle, which Hobbes thought he could solve. Hobbes knew practically nothing of mathematics until middle age. I quote a well-known passage from Aubrey:

He was 40 years old before he looked on geometry; which happened accidentally. Being in a gentleman's library, Euclid's Elements lay open, and 'twas the 47[th proposition of Book I]. He read the proposition. *By G—*, said he, ... *this is impossible!* So he reads the demonstration of it, which referred him back to such a proposition; which proposition he read. That referred him back to another, which he also read. *Et sic deinceps* [and so on] that at last he was demonstratively convinced of that truth. This made him in love with geometry.

Hobbes's duties as tutor to young noblemen took him abroad to France. There he got to know some of the leading continental thinkers, and influenced by their interest in natural science he studied physics and physiology, and began to think about questions of metaphysics, especially problems of perception. He made a special journey to Italy in order to meet Galileo, whose ideas were to make a profound impression on his own thought.

He returned to England in 1637. His contact with Descartes, Galileo, and other philosophers and scientists on the Continent had inspired him to plan a comprehensive philosophical work in three parts, the first on Body (i.e. matter), the second on Man (i.e. physiology and psychology), and the third on the Citizen or the Body Politic (i.e. political philosophy). In all three parts, one concept was to provide the basis of explanation – the concept of motion. Hobbes's materialist metaphysics, with the idea of motion as the unitary concept, is of some interest in the history of general philosophy; but he made his greatest impact in the history of political philosophy. Ethical theory comes into Hobbes's consideration as a necessary part of his political theory.

Hobbes says in the last paragraph of *Leviathan* that he was moved to write about political philosophy owing to the civil disturbances of the time, and that having completed the task he can now return to his 'interrupted speculation of bodies natural' (i.e. to natural science and metaphysics). It is certainly true that Hobbes's special interest in political theory was due to the troubled political situation, and this is what enabled him to produce a political philosophy of the first importance. To be a great philosopher it is not enough to have great talent. The talent must also be faced with an important real-life problem. Great metaphysical philosophy arises when there is a severe intellectual strain in reconciling old and new bodies of thought; for instance, when a striking advance in scientific knowledge seems to show that traditional beliefs, of religious doctrine or simply of common experience, are illusory. Similarly, great moral and political philosophy arises when traditional ideas seem to be upset by new experiences; for instance, when the travels of the Greek Sophists showed them the variety of moral and legal codes and so led them to doubt whether there were any absolute or objective principles in morals; or again, when the defeat of democratic Athens by aristocratic Sparta led Plato to doubt the values of the democratic ideal; and again, when the threat and the reality of civil war led Hobbes to doubt the wisdom of limited or divided authority. Hobbes's interest in politics had shown itself in his first publication, a translation of Thucydides put out in 1628. Thucydides' work is a history of the war between Athens and Sparta, and Thucydides is plainly led, by the experience of living through that war, to lay the blame on the democratic system of government at Athens – as Plato was to do after him; indeed Plato was, in this respect, following up and strengthening what he regarded as the lesson of Thucydides. Hobbes took a similar view. Political insecurity shows the need for strong government. The 1620s had seen several clashes between Charles I and Parliament, culminating in the Petition of Right in 1628, the year in which Hobbes's translation of Thucydides was published. Hobbes says that he foresaw the possibility of civil war and hoped that a knowledge of Thucydides' history would help to prevent it.

When Hobbes returned to England from France in 1637, the dangers of civil disturbance were more apparent, and especially of civil disturbance due to religious conflict. This explains why Hobbes wants to subordinate the authority of the Church to that of the State. In 1637 the attempt to impose a Book of Common Prayer on the Scots caused a riot in Edinburgh, followed by the Covenant of 1638, and this led directly to the Great Rebellion. When Charles I asked Parliament in 1640 for money to raise an army against the Scots, he was faced with the demands of Pym and Hampden for limitation of the king's powers. These were the circumstances in which Hobbes wrote his first political work, *The Elements of Law*,* and expanded it into the treatise called *De Cive* (The Citizen), published in 1642. *Leviathan* was published in 1651, after the execution of Charles I (1649), and it was alleged by some that Hobbes wrote this work to flatter Cromwell and to enable himself to return from France, where he had been since 1640. But although *Leviathan* is Hobbes's masterpiece, being more brilliant in style than *De Cive*, the political doctrines of the two books are almost exactly the same. In Hobbes's view, it was immaterial who held the power, so long as it was absolute power, held securely.

In Paris he had been recommended in 1646 as tutor to the Prince of Wales, who afterwards was to reign as Charles II. When *Leviathan* was published, Hobbes sent a copy to Charles, who, however, forbade Hobbes to come into his presence on learning that the clergy were very much against the book. The last of the four parts of *Leviathan* includes a vicious attack on the Church of Rome, and in consequence the Roman Catholic clergy of France were even more incensed against Hobbes than the English clergy. He therefore left France at the end of 1651 and returned to England. Soon after the Restoration of the Monarchy in 1660, Charles, who remained fond of his former tutor, happened to see Hobbes in London, invited him back to the Court, and promised him a

* Copies of the manuscript of this work were circulated among Hobbes's friends, but it was not published until later. The first part was originally published, without Hobbes's authority, under the title *Human Nature* in 1650; a second edition of it, revised and approved by Hobbes, appeared in 1651. The properly political subject-matter of *The Elements of Law* came in Part II, which Hobbes published in 1650 (after *Human Nature*) under the title *De Corpore Politico: or the Elements of Law, moral and politic*.

pension of £100 a year, which he sometimes forgot to pay. Aubrey tells us that 'the wits at Court were wont to bait' Hobbes. 'But he feared none of them, and would make his part good. The king would call him *the bear*: here comes the bear to be baited.'

In 1666 *Leviathan* and *De Cive* were censured by Parliament, and a Bill to punish atheism, doubtless aimed at Hobbes, was brought into the House of Commons. The Bill was eventually dropped, probably through the influence of Charles, but Hobbes was forbidden to publish anything in England. So he published his future works in Holland. The last of his books appeared when he was 87. Hobbes was a vigorous man and took plenty of physical exercise. He lived to the ripe old age of 91, dying on 4 December 1679.

The popular idea that Hobbes was an atheist is intelligible, but it is not easy to say whether the description can properly be applied to him. On the whole I think it cannot. Hobbes has a definite view of God, and I think he holds it sincerely. He is a materialist and his idea of God is certainly not the traditional one. Yet he can always find scriptural precedent for his views. It is plain from the latter half of *Leviathan* that Hobbes knows the Bible extremely well, and he makes quite a case for the view that the original language of the Bible should be interpreted in accordance with a materialist metaphysics. His particular conception of God, as a being of *irresistible power*, whose actions are to be justified on that ground alone, is mainly derived from the Book of Job. This seems to have been Hobbes's favourite book of the Bible. The name 'Leviathan' is taken from the Book of Job, where the great monster leviathan is called 'a king over all the children of pride'. Hobbes quotes this passage at the end of Chapter 28 of *Leviathan*, beginning his quotation with the words 'There is nothing, on earth, to be compared with him'. The original edition of *Leviathan* has a famous pictorial title-page, at the top of which the State or sovereign is depicted as a king made up of the multitude of citizens; and above his head is the Latin motto from the Book of Job, *Non est potestas Super Terram quae Comparetur ei* (There is no power on earth to be compared with him). This is why Hobbes elsewhere (in Chapter 17) calls the State a 'mortal God'. The immortal God is to be defined in terms of *power*: there is no power in the whole universe to be compared with him. So too the artificial imitation of God, the 'mortal God' that is the State, requires to have as much power as possible.

I shall end this account of Hobbes's life with two more quotations from Aubrey, one about Hobbes's intellectual habits, the other relating to his character.

'He had very few books', says Aubrey. 'He had read much, if one considers his long life; but his concentration was much more than his reading. He was wont to say that if he had read as much as other men, he should have known no more than other men.'

My second quotation is worth remembering in connection with Hobbes's egoistic psychology. A man may give an egoistic interpretation of human motives without being selfish in his actions.

He was very charitable to those that were the true objects of his bounty. One time, I remember, going in the Strand, a poor and infirm old man craved his alms. He, beholding him with eyes of pity and compassion, put his hand in his pocket and gave him 6d [a substantial sum in those days]. Said a divine that stood by, Would you have done this, if it had not been Christ's command? Yea, said he. Why? quoth the other. Because, said he, I was in pain to consider the miserable condition of the old man; and now my alms, giving him some relief, doth also ease me.

Chapter II

Problem and Method

P2,3

The problem which set Hobbes thinking about moral and political philosophy was how to avoid civil war and civil disorder. I said in Chapter 1 that Hobbes, like Plato, took to heart the lesson of Thucydides about the great war between Athens and Sparta. Hobbes was led to embark on political philosophy for the same reason as Plato, and it is worth pursuing the analogy a little, because I rather think that the same reason applies to all important new ventures in political thought. That reason is the experience of political upheaval.

Plato had seen the downfall of the Athenian empire, a swift change from democracy to tyranny ('the Thirty Tyrants') and to oligarchy, with discord and disruption. Not understanding the wider forces at work in the Greek world, Plato attributed the troubles of his time to the form of political constitution which Athens had enjoyed, democracy. Plato thought democracy was responsible for the weaknesses of the Athenian city-state, and therefore he attacked it, thinking that a more authoritarian form of government would have ensured stability. Plato judged from his own, necessarily limited, experience and therefore attacked the democracy he had known. If he had lived later, he would probably have taken a different view. This is not to say that Plato's political philosophy is of interest only to his contemporaries. It is important to see the causes of a man's views, but an understanding of the historical *causes* does not make it unnecessary to consider the *reasons* that he gives for his conclusions. Plato's attack on democracy is supported by pretty forceful reasons. Just because it is the effect of Plato's experience of political convulsion, it represents a fundamental rethinking of moral and political issues, and presents us with important problems. If we disagree with Plato's solutions, he gives us the difficult task of finding better solutions and of answering his objections to the democratic way of life.

The same is true of Hobbes. Hobbes's political philosophy is his answer to the threat and the reality of civil war. His problem was to consider how such civil war and turmoil might be avoided. Like Plato, he decided that absolute obedience on the part of subjects was the only way to ensure political stability, and his political theory is an attempt prove the necessity of absolute rule and virtually absolute obedience. Just as Plato was unable to see the political fortunes of Athens as part of a wider movement of change, so Hobbes was unable to see the rebellion of Parliament against Charles I as part of the general dissolution of the medieval structure of thought and society, a dissolution of which his own work is a symptom. Hobbes approved of the revolt against papal authority and of the revolt against Aristotelian conceptions of science; but he did not see that the revolt against the divine right of kings was, like the Renaissance and the Reformation, part of the crumbling of the medieval structure of society, in which every man had his appointed place, subject to authority. Hobbes wants to keep authority in morals and politics while discarding it for belief. But the new appeal to reason in science and religion, which he supports, carried with it the authority of the individual's conscience in other matters too.

Still, if we disagree with Hobbes's solution of his political problem, he gives us, like Plato, the difficult task of finding a better solution. In Hobbes's time the problem was posed by civil war. In our time it is posed by the danger of international war. Hobbes's definitions of war and peace, in Chapter 13 of *Leviathan*, may have sounded cynical in more secure times. In our own era of so-called 'cold war', they ring more truly:

> For WAR, consisteth not in battle only, or the act of fighting; but in a tract of time, wherein the will to contend by battle is sufficiently known: and therefore the notion of *time*, is to be considered in the nature of war; as it is in the nature of weather. For as the nature of foul weather, lieth not in a shower or two of rain; but in an inclination thereto of many days together: so the nature of war, consisteth not in actual fighting; but in the known disposition thereto, during all the time there is no assurance to the contrary. All other time is PEACE.

Hobbes tells us that the only way to put an end to the state of war is to form a commonwealth, either by agreement or by force of arms, and then to have in that commonwealth an absolute sovereign claiming virtually absolute obedience. Without this, there will be no security. We may put Hobbes's problem and his proposed solution into modern terms by saying that Hobbes would tell us that international war and international insecurity can be avoided only by a World State possessing absolute authority. It might come into being by agreement or by conquest. Hobbes would insist that its authority must be absolute. If we do not like this conclusion, we must examine his reasons, and also ask ourselves what alternative solution we can offer, based on different reasons.

17

Modern philosophy begins in the seventeenth century and is as revolutionary as those other harbingers of the modern world, the Renaissance, the Reformation, and the rise of modern science. It is fashionable to say that there has been a revolution in philosophy in the twentieth century. Whether this is a sound judgement we must leave to future generations. We need have no hesitation in saying that there was a revolution in philosophy in the seventeenth century. Descartes is responsible for initiating the revolution in the philosophy of knowledge (epistemology and metaphysics), Hobbes in the philosophy of practice (moral and political philosophy). With both, the revolution was due to the new scientific movement. What is particularly novel about Hobbes's philosophy is not the doctrine of political absolutism, but the method whereby he attempts to prove his doctrines. That method is what he takes to be the scientific method. Hobbes's philosophy is an attempt to apply the methods and fundamental concepts of physics to the study of man, both as an individual and as a citizen. Although there had been previous theories of society and the State, Hobbes was the first to make a deliberate use, in social studies, of the model of physical science. For this reason I think it is fair to call him the inventor of social *science* as that term has been understood in the modern world.

There are two ways in which Hobbes tries to make the study of society scientific. First, he uses the scientific method of causal explanation. Secondly (and this is more radical), he treats the sciences of man and society as themselves part of physics. This second and more radical point is the key to Hobbes's materialist metaphysics. At the moment I am concerned only with the first point, causal explanation; and since I propose to consider Hobbes's use of causal explanation in his political theory, I shall mainly confine myself to his most brilliant work, *Leviathan*.

In the seventeenth century no distinction was commonly made between the terms 'science' and 'philosophy'. The one word was Latin, the other Greek, that was all. Both represented ordered inquiry. Such inquiry into the workings of the material world of nature was called Natural Philosophy (still retained as the name for physics in some universities); inquiry into the workings of the mind was called Mental Philosophy (the old name for what we now call psychology); inquiry into human action was called Moral Philosophy. In *Leviathan* Hobbes is chiefly concerned with inquiry about human action in ordered society, commonwealth or *civitas*, and this he calls Civil Philosophy.

Hobbes requires of philosophy that it should pursue what he takes to be the correct method, of causal explanation, and also that it should be useful. At the beginning of Chapter 46 of *Leviathan*, he defines philosophy as follows:

By PHILOSOPHY, is understood *the knowledge acquired by reasoning, from the manner of the generation of any thing, to the properties; or from the properties, to some possible way of generation of the same; to the end to be able to produce, as far as matter, and human force permit, such effects, as human life requireth.* So the geometrician, from the construction of figures, findeth out many properties thereof; and from the properties, new ways of their construction, by reasoning; to the end to be able to measure land, and water; and for infinite other uses.

Hobbes then attacks ancient philosophy on the ground that it has produced no useful results, and again refers to the value of geometry:

But what has been the utility of those schools? what science is there at this day acquired by their readings and disputings? . . . The natural philosophy of those schools, was rather a dream than science, and set forth in senseless and insignificant language; which cannot be avoided by those that will teach philosophy, without having first attained great knowledge in geometry. For nature worketh by motion; the ways, and degrees whereof cannot be known, without the knowledge of the proportions and properties of lines, and figures.

The method, then, is the method of geometry. Here, as in his reference to nature working by motion, Hobbes is following Galileo, who had said this (*The Assayer*, §6):

Philosophy is written in that vast book which stands forever open before our eyes, I mean the universe; but it cannot be read until we have learnt the language and become familiar with the characters in which it is written. It is written in mathematical language, and the letters are triangles, circles, and other geometrical figures, without which means it is humanly impossible to understand a single word.

It is true that the physicist applies geometry to his study of matter. But one may well wonder how geometry is supposed to consist of *causal* reasoning; and since *Leviathan* is primarily concerned with civil philosophy, one may wonder still more what analogy there is between that and geometry. The answer to both queries depends on Hobbes's view of definitions. Hobbes holds that a good definition, in geometry or in anything else, states how the thing being defined is made up. It gives a method of generation or construction, a possible cause. For instance, you can define a circle as a plane figure bounded by a single line, called the circumference, which is everywhere equidistant from a point within it, called the centre; or alternatively, you can define a circle as the figure produced by one end of a straight line moving continuously while the other end remains fixed. Hobbes would prefer the second definition, because this explains how a circle is produced or generated, how it is caused. Now deductive reasoning proceeds from definitions; the reasoner sees what is implied by his definitions. And if his definitions describe the *causes* of what he is talking about, the consequences of those definitions describe the *effects* of the causes. So Hobbes does not mean that geometry itself can be used in studying human behaviour. He means that the method of reasoning used by the geometer is the proper scientific method, to be applied to any study that aims at being scientific. That method is reasoning from causes to effects, or from effects to possible causes. If you are reasoning from cause to effect, the cause must be described by a definition, and then the consequences of the definition will describe the effects. If you do not know the cause, but do know the effects, you can reason from the effects to a *possible* cause, by analysing the effects and seeing what could produce them. I have said that definition describes a cause. But if you do not know the cause, and have to start from the effects, you can only get to know these by experience. Then you can use reasoning to determine whether the definition of any suggested cause implies, as consequences, the effects which you know have occurred.

Hobbes's method is applied to civil philosophy in the following way. He has experience of two kinds of effects: civil strife or disorder, and stable or ordered society. He asks what are the causes of each, and he finds that human nature can be shown to be a possible cause in both cases. He therefore carefully defines the elements in human nature that can give rise to these effects, building up his definitions and relating them together in such a way as to show how strife or war between men may come about, and how ordered society may come about. The point of this inquiry is that the state of war is undesirable, and ordered society desirable. Hobbes must therefore show us also how the desirable thing can be maintained. This he does by making use of his causal explanations. Disorder or war is due to man's natural desire for power, his ambition or 'pride'. Organized society is due to man's desire for security, his fear of death. To obtain security, man needs protection from his fellows, protection that is afforded by the power of the State. But this protection can be exercised securely only if the State has virtually absolute authority, i.e. only if the subjects give to the State their almost complete obedience. At the end of *Leviathan*, Hobbes sums up his doctrine as showing 'the mutual relation between protection and obedience'. His philosophy, then, has demonstrated relations of cause and effect, and it is useful for human life, since it is intended to sustain obedience to the State, and so to sustain that protection which men need.

In the course of this scientific 'civil' or political philosophy, we are also given a scientific moral philosophy. At the end of Chapter 15 of *Leviathan*, Hobbes says that the only true moral philosophy is the science of the laws of nature. Laws of nature, for Hobbes, are rational rules for self-preservation. They are rules which we can reason out as the only way to preserve our lives, the human condition being what it is. We reason out these rules when we see where our irrational human nature leads us, namely, to a state of war, in which the life of no one is secure. It is the laws of nature that tell us to set up, or to keep in existence, an organized State, and to give to that State our virtually complete obedience. A study of the laws of nature, therefore, is a scientific study. For it is a study of causal connections between human nature and civil society; and it is a useful study, since it brings into a clearer light the reasons why we should obey the State.

Chapter III

Metaphysics and Psychology

The fundamental idea of Hobbes's metaphysics, i.e. his theory of reality, is very simple indeed: the world consists of matter in motion. So far as the physical world is concerned, this idea is intelligible enough. Galileo had given natural philosophy a new and evidently fruitful start by dealing with physical objects in terms of motion. We now think of classical mechanics as founded on Newton's three laws of motion, but these are generalizations of laws that Galileo discovered. All very well for inanimate matter; but what about life and mind? Hobbes's metaphysical theory comes down to this: there is no difference ultimately between matter, life, and mind; all of them are matter. Galileo's laws apply to everything in the world, for everything is matter in motion. Hence Hobbes is a materialist in the strictest sense. He extends Galileo's idea beyond the limited realm studied by physics and applies it to everything. This kind of move is typical of the metaphysician. He takes a concept which has proved fruitful in one field and extends its application as widely as possible.

Let us now see how Hobbes tries to do this with the idea of matter in motion. He was probably led to it by putting together the work of Galileo and that of Harvey, the man who discovered the circulation of the blood. Harvey published his discovery in 1628, and he describes how he first thought of the hypothesis in these words: 'I began to think whether there might not be a motion as it were in a circle.' *Motion* in a *circle*. Harvey is applying, in his physiological inquiries, a *geometrical* notion such as is used in physics. It is likely that this gave Hobbes the idea that physiology is essentially the same sort of thing as physics, a science in which geometrical notions are applied to matter in motion. Next comes Hobbes's crucial step. He formulates the idea that *life* is simply a form of *internal* motion in matter. Inanimate matter requires an external force to alter its motion; a billiard ball rolling along the table has its motion altered by the force of another billiard ball which strikes it. Living things are different, in that their motion can be changed by a cause within themselves. Now the circulation of the blood, and perhaps the Old Testament statement (Leviticus 17:14) that the life of all flesh is its blood, suggest to Hobbes that life simply is an internal motion in the organ and just as the motion of one billiard ball can be affected by the motion of another, so the outwardly observable movements of an organism can be affected by the *internal* movements which we do not normally see. The causes of the behaviour, of the observable movements, of an organism are the same as the causes of the observable movements of inanimate matter, namely, the force of matter in motion.

Hobbes therefore thinks of animal behaviour, including human behaviour, as a form of matter in motion, caused by internal physiological motion in the organs of the body. Such internal physiological motion he calls 'vital motion', i.e. motion that constitutes life. The externally observable movements of the organism, which are caused by vital motions, he calls 'animal motion' or 'voluntary motion'. (We shall see later his reasons for the alternative name of 'voluntary motion'.) This then is how Hobbes applies the materialist hypothesis to the concept of life, to the behaviour of organisms as well as to inanimate matter.

What of mind or consciousness? Here Hobbes is faced with a more difficult problem. His apparent success in correlating physics with physiology, in joining the work of Galileo to that of Harvey, led him to think that the same move could be extended to psychology. Let us look for a moment at his account of perception. When I perceive something, according to Hobbes, what really happens is all a matter of physics and physiology. An instance of matter in motion comes into contact with an organ of the body. This causes a change in the movements of the organ, which in turn cause a change in the movements of the nerves. The motion in the nerves continues to the brain and the heart; and since the heart has its own system of forceful motion, the impact of the new motion communicated from the outside body meets with resistance (just as the impact of one moving billiard ball on another brings out a resistance in the second moving body). The resistance of the heart Hobbes describes, in Chapter I of *Leviathan*, as a 'counter-pressure, or endeavour of the heart, to deliver it self'. That is to say, the internal organ exerts force outwards, to counteract the force coming inwards. Now this 'endeavour' or movement outwards, because it is outwards, 'seems' to be something outside. And this 'seeming' or 'phantasm' or 'fancy' is what we call sensation. We seem to perceive something outside us. When, for example, I look at the paper on which these words are printed, or if I grasp the paper, what is really going on, according to Hobbes, is the pressure or force of material motions from the paper to my eye or hand and then within my body. But it seems to me as if I were aware of something outside myself. What I am aware of is in fact a 'fancy', an 'appearance', a by-product of the physiological movements inside my body. So that consciousness, for Hobbes, is mere appearance. What goes on in the body is real; what we call mental experiences are simply appearances of bodily motion. Mind or conscious experience is not real at all; it is appearance. What is real is the bodily matter in motion.

Having given a materialistic account of sensation or perception, as an appearance of physiological motion, Hobbes can proceed to build up a picture of cognitive experience founded upon sensation. Imagination, mental imagery, is 'decaying' or fading sense. Memory is just another name for the same thing, but we call it imagination when we attend to the fancies, the images, themselves; and we call it memory when we attend to the fact that the images simply are the fading remnants of sense. Imagination joined with the use of words constitutes thinking. The details of Hobbes's account of thinking are of interest for epistemology, but since I am more concerned with his moral and political philosophy I do not need to take any further Hobbes's views of the cognitive capacities of the mind.

We can turn now to his account of the conative and affective faculties, i.e. his view of desire, volition, and feeling. Here again the experience of consciousness, according to Hobbes, is merely the appearance of bodily motion.

It works like this. Suppose I feel hungry. This is a conscious feeling. We shall all agree that when I am hungry my stomach is in a different state from that in which it is when I do not feel hungry. According to Hobbes, all that is really going on is the movements in the nerves and organs of the stomach; the vital motion is slowing down. But these movements 'appear' in the mind as a feeling of hunger, a form of pain or 'uneasiness'. Now suppose that, feeling hungry, I go to the kitchen and get some bread and cheese; I eat it and then feel satisfied. We should normally say that I went to the kitchen for food *because* I felt hungry, and that afterwards I feel satisfied *because* I have eaten. We regard the feeling of hunger as the cause of my going into the kitchen for bread and cheese, and we regard the eating of food as the cause of the subsequent feeling of satisfaction. On this commonsensical view of the situation, a psychological experience causes an action or, if you like, a piece of bodily behaviour, what Hobbes would call 'animal motion'; and another action or instance of 'animal motion' causes a further psychological experience. The causal process can go from mind to body and from body to mind.

Now let us think of this from a materialistic point of view, omitting all references to feelings or other mental experiences, and instead tracing the pattern of causes simply by reference to matter in motion, including both 'vital motion' and 'animal motion'. This is how Hobbes looks at it.

The vital motion, the movements in the nerves and organs of the stomach, cause the animal motions of walking into the kitchen, taking food, and eating it. As the food passes into the stomach, it causes new vital motions. The organs and nerves are now in a different state from their earlier one. The vital motion has been speeded up, running smoothly again. This is all that really happens. But the real vital motions 'appear' in the mind as feelings. The original physiological movements appear in the mind as a feeling of hunger; and at the end of the process the speeding up of the physiological movements appears in the mind as a feeling of satisfaction.

Since desire is really physiological movement, which causes bodily movement, Hobbes reasons further that the physiological movements must be the 'first beginnings' of the bodily movement. According to this account, when I desire to eat food, what is really happening is that my nerves and muscles are beginning those movements which will soon be outwardly observable in the movement of my limbs taking me to the kitchen. Desire therefore is really the first small beginnings of action; and action is bodily movement. This movement can be towards a thing or away from a thing. When it is towards a thing (as in my example of moving towards the bread and cheese in the kitchen), we give to the 'small beginnings' the name of desire or appetite. When the bodily movement is away from a thing (as, for instance, when I run in from the rain), we call the 'small beginnings' by the name of aversion. I dislike rain, I don't want to be soaked by the rain. Not wanting, or aversion, is the small beginnings of movement away from a thing. Appetite (or desire) and aversion are specific forms of 'endeavour', which is Hobbes's name for the small beginnings of motion in general. It is worth noting that the Latin words from which 'appetite' and 'aversion' are derived have definite connotations of moving towards or away from a thing, of seeking and of turning away. Hobbes read and wrote Latin with ease, and the connotations of Latin terms often influence the way in which he understands a concept.

We should next see how desire and aversion are connected with pleasure and pain. The feeling of hunger, we have learned, is 'really' a bodily state. It is a state of the stomach which, if not dealt with, will eventually produce starvation and death. When I am hungry, my vital processes are going slowly, they are liable to run down. When I have eaten food, my vital processes can run smoothly again. Hobbes holds that the feelings of pleasure and pain are the mental appearances of the vital processes according as they are running smoothly or not. Consequently, whenever something happens which impedes the vital processes, the impeding appears in the mind as a painful feeling, a warning that life is in danger. On the other hand, whenever something happens

which assists the vital processes, this change appears in the mind as a feeling of pleasure, a sign that life or vital motion is going along nicely. Hunger is therefore felt as painful, and repletion is felt as pleasant or a satisfaction. And since I know from past experience that the eating of food produces pleasure in this way, I anticipate the pleasure when I desire the food. So the object of a desire is thought of as pleasant, and similarly the object of aversion is thought of as painful or unpleasant.

Now it is characteristic of a living thing that it endeavours to go on living. Hobbes probably links this too with a principle of Galileo, the principle of inertia, that a piece of matter, if left to itself, tends to continue in the state of motion or rest in which it now is. However that may be, a living thing does have the tendency to go on living, and so it behaves in ways that will assist this tendency. In a conscious being, like man, the tendency of the organism appears in the mind as a desire for self-preservation; and the other side of this coin is an aversion from death. For Hobbes, the desire for self-preservation or aversion from death is the fundamental motive of human conduct. Further, since pleasure is the sign of heightened vitality and pain is the sign of diminished vitality, the desire to go on living and to avoid death implies a desire for pleasure and an aversion from pain.

From these simple foundations Hobbes builds up a quite complicated account of human motives and feelings. It is stated summarily in Chapter 6 of *Leviathan*, where the concise and epigrammatic forms of Hobbes's definitions have their own fascination. Hobbes had previously given a much fuller account in the latter half of *Human Nature*; and although some of the definitions in *Leviathan* show an improvement over those of *Human Nature*, it is well worth going back to the earlier book in order to appreciate the ingenuity of Hobbes's psychology, built up as it is on the basis of a strictly materialist metaphysics and in accordance with Hobbes's recommended method of proceeding by way of definitions and the consequences of definitions. Let me give a couple of examples. Hobbes defines hope as desire for a thing together with the opinion that we are likely to attain it, while despair is desire for a thing with the opinion that we are not likely to attain it. Fear he defines as aversion from a thing together with the opinion that we are not likely to avoid it, i.e. together with the opinion that we are likely to receive hurt from it. Hurt or harm is of course a species of evil, and Hobbes defines good and evil also in terms of desire and aversion. What we call good is simply the object of desire, and what we call evil is simply the object of aversion. In Hobbes's view, therefore, to call a thing good is tantamount to saying that we desire that thing, and to call a thing evil is tantamount to saying that we feel aversion in regard to that thing.

If action is caused by the physiological motion (endeavour) which appears either as desire or as aversion, what are we to say of the will? According to Hobbes, the 'will' is simply a name for that endeavour which immediately precedes an action; and we apply the name when there has been a process of deliberation, which Hobbes explains as simply the alternation of various motives, of appetites and aversions of various kinds, some being inclinations to go one way, others being inclinations to go the other way. Hobbes thinks of the will as the result of a balance of forces. He is of course dealing with action in mechanistic terms, in terms of the laws of mechanics, of matter in motion. He is therefore a determinist. When there is a conflict of endeavours, a conflict of forces, some impelling in one direction, others impelling in a contrary direction, the action that a man finally takes will be determined by the balance of forces. There cannot therefore be 'free will', i.e. the possibility of acting against the greatest weight of inclination. What we call the will is simply the last desire or aversion that shows itself just before the overt animal motion takes place, it is the particular instance of endeavour that is the immediate cause of the action. This is why Hobbes calls action 'animal motion or voluntary motion'. In animals which possess consciousness, the cause of animal motion appears in the mind as desire or will (Hobbes takes the word 'will' to mean more or less the same as wanting, no doubt again influenced by the fact that both could be expressed in Latin by the verb *volo*); and therefore the action may be described as being caused by the will or as being voluntary. We can translate the word 'voluntary' sometimes as meaning willed, sometimes as meaning in accordance with our wishes. Hobbes takes 'voluntary' to mean caused by our own desire. You may feel inclined to ask how Hobbes can distinguish between voluntary and involuntary behaviour when he denies that there is any such thing as free will. He holds that form of determinism which is called self-determinism. All action is necessary, but not all action is necessitated by external causes. Liberty or freedom is to be contrasted with external compulsion. If I am compelled by prison bars to stay where I am, I am not free, I am not at liberty. But if I stay in one particular room because I want to, or even because I am afraid that I shall suffer some unpleasant experience if I go out, then I act of my own volition. The cause of my action is internal, not external; it is desire or fear (a form of aversion), and not an external force. Hence, in Hobbes's usage, it is voluntary or free, as contrasted with action that is compelled by an external cause.

Hobbes's account of psychology and of human motives is oversimplified, but it is a really remarkable attempt to build up the whole picture from as few premises as possible. Although his account is open to serious criticism, we should remember that it is a sound principle in science (and in philosophy too) to make one's scheme of explanation as simple as possible. That is why Hobbes does what he does. He not only makes psychology simple. He also tries to reduce psychology to physiology, and to reduce physiology to physics. Everything is matter in motion, and the motion everywhere takes place according to the simple laws of mechanics.

Chapter IV

Morals and Politics – I

Now that we have some idea of Hobbes's simple mechanistic picture of the world of nature, including man, we are in a position to consider his theory of morals and politics. In this chapter I shall give a general outline of that theory, and in the following chapter I shall consider in more detail some points of special interest. We should recall in the first instance that Hobbes's political philosophy is designed to meet a problem of real life, and that his moral philosophy is introduced only as a necessary part of the solution to the political problem.

Hobbes's problem, it will be remembered, is to discover how to maintain a stable ordered society and how to avoid disorder or civil war. To deal with the problem 'scientifically' he must find the causes of each of these situations. He will then be in a position to consider how we may make it possible for the causes of ordered society to operate and for the causes of disorder to be overcome. The cause of ordered society is the desire for security; the main causes of disorder are competition, distrust, and 'glory' (enjoyment of power). If security is to be maintained, and competition and 'glory' restrained, there must be a power with absolute authority to prevent men from harming each other; they must be *subject* to a *sovereign* power. How can they be persuaded to accept this? By showing them the reasons why they should obey the State. Hobbes is thus led to expound the grounds of political obligation; and to do this he must show the grounds of obligation generally. That is to say, he is led to give us a theory of obligation, a theory of morals.

In order to explain Hobbes's theory of obligation, and indeed his political theory as a whole, it is necessary to emphasize a distinction which is of key importance in his work, the distinction between the natural and the artificial. This distinction is drawn in the very first words of *Leviathan*, and it runs throughout the work. Nature, or the natural, is what we find. Art, or the artificial, is what we make. The world of nature is not made by man; he just finds it, and it includes himself. For God, who has made the world, the world is artificial. Now art, human art, can to some degree imitate nature, the art of God. For instance, Hobbes defines a living thing, an animal, as a piece of matter

29

that has the power of moving itself. A man, or a dog, is a natural animal. But what of a piece of matter that has been artificially contrived to move itself? An automatic machine, such as a clockwork train, for instance? This answers to the definition of an animal, but it is artificial, not natural. It is an artificial animal, an imitation of a natural animal. Hobbes thinks of the State as an artificial animal, indeed an artificial man. It is artificial, not so much because it can be set up by a social contract (for that is not the only way whereby a State, in Hobbes's view, can come into existence), but because it needs to be kept in being *deliberately*, just as one has to keep winding up the clockwork train. If the train is just left to itself, if power is not deliberately applied when power is needed, the train will run down, it will 'die', i.e. it will cease to be an 'animal'. So with the State. If it is left alone, it will drift into civil war or anarchy, it will cease to be an organized State. Hence Hobbes calls civil war the 'death' of the commonwealth. In this sense, therefore, anarchy or war is natural, while organized commonwealth is artificial. And just because the State is artificial, while anarchy is natural, men need to be told what they must do to keep the State in being.

We may say, then, that anarchy (the sort of thing that occurs in civil war, or any kind of war) is natural, while organized society is artificial. Let us now look with greater precision for possible causes of each. If anarchy or war between men is natural, it is likely, or at least possible, that the cause lies in human nature. Hobbes thinks we know by experience that human nature is predominantly egoistic. Men are mainly out for their own interests. That is why they compete and fight. But why is human nature egoistic? Because the natural tendency of any organism is to preserve its own life. In a state of nature, a man desires self-preservation and will do anything that seems to him necessary for self-preservation. Furthermore, it does not make sense to say that he is obliged to refrain from such actions. For what motive could he have to refrain? His fundamental motive is the desire for self-preservation, and so he cannot have an effective motive to act in ways that he thinks will militate against his own preservation. If he cannot have such a motive, it does not make sense to say that he is obliged so to act. He has a right to do anything which he thinks will conduce to his preservation; and this right has no limits if he cannot trust others to live and let live. To say that a man has a right to do something, is to say that he has no obligation to refrain. In a state of nature, every man has a right to all things. He may do whatever he chooses. This is his natural right.

The desire for self-preservation gives rise to a desire for pleasure, since pleasure is the appearance in consciousness of what conduces to life. Conversely there is an aversion from pain, pain being the mental appearance of what conduces to death. According to Hobbes, man's desire for continued preservation leads him to desire not only pleasure now but a store of pleasure for the future, since that means a store of continued life in the future. How can one lay up a store of future pleasure? By acquiring power. Power is the means to satisfy our desires. Therefore every man naturally desires power and more power, 'a perpetual and restless desire of power after power, that ceaseth only in death' (*Leviathan*, Chapter 11). If one person had power so great that no one could resist him, he would be master of all. This is the position of God. God is irresistible, in consequence of which he has the right of dominion (*Leviathan*, Chapter 31). But among men in a natural state, none has the ability to attain for himself powers so great that he can have dominion over all. Roughly speaking, all men are equal in their capacity to acquire power. One man may be physically stronger than another, but the second may be more cunning and so able to outwit the first by stratagem if not by physical strength. No man has enough power to compel all to do his will. All are roughly equal in power, and all can exercise their unlimited natural right.

What is the result? If no man is my master, equally no man is my slave. My neighbour is as strong as I, and as self-assertive as I. We fear each other, and we are liable to come into conflict with each other because we desire the same things. No one is strong enough to kill, or make himself master of, everyone else. So all go in mutual fear and suspicion, and from time to time there will be battles, in which any man is liable to lose his life. The natural state of mankind is a state of war, 'where every man is enemy to every man'. There is 'continual fear, and danger of violent death; and the life of man, solitary, poor, nasty, brutish, and short' (*Leviathan*, Chapter 13). Here, then, is the state of anarchy, into which human society tends to drift if left to take its natural course. Hobbes has shown that its cause lies in human nature, the desire for self-preservation, leading to competition.

Fortunately, this situation carries within it its own remedy. The fundamental cause of the behaviour that leads to the state of war can also supply the cause of extrication from this predicament. For the fundamental cause is the desire for self-preservation, which implies an aversion from death. But the state of war, into which men are led by their natural desires, is a condition in which life is nasty, brutish, and *short*. The result that is reached is the opposite of what was aimed at. Men aim at continued preservation of life, and find themselves in a situation where they are likely to lose their lives. They have a natural aversion from death, but are in a position where they are unlikely to avoid death for long. It will be recalled that Hobbes defined fear as aversion from a thing together with the opinion that one is not likely to avoid it. In the state of war, therefore, men are faced with the fear of

31

death. They have a natural aversion from death but are in a situation where they can see they are unlikely to avoid death for long. This motive, the fear of death, which arises in the state of war, supplies the cause of putting an end to that state.

Being moved to end the natural state of war, a rational man can see that he should seek the opposite, a state of peace. This piece of reasoning, which prescribes the means to secure our fundamental aim of self-preservation, Hobbes calls a 'precept', or 'general rule', or 'theorem', of reason (*Leviathan*, Chapters 14–15). He also calls it the first law of nature. A law of nature differs from the right of nature. The right of nature is what we *may* do, what we are at liberty to do, in order to preserve our lives. A law of nature states an obligation or a precept or rule; it tells us what we *should* do, what we are obliged to do, in order to preserve our lives. To use the language that was later to be introduced in ethical theory by Immanuel Kant, a law of nature is a hypothetical imperative; it prescribes a means to our own interest. The particular methods whereby we may carry out the first and fundamental law of nature, namely, to seek peace, are listed by Hobbes as further laws of nature; they are means to peace, which is itself a means to self-preservation.

Hobbes explains, at the end of Chapter 15 of *Leviathan*, that the word 'law' should properly be applied only to a command issued by someone with a right to be obeyed. He adds that the description which he has given earlier of the 'laws of nature' does not strictly justify the use of the word 'law'. But, he adds, if we look upon these precepts of reason as something communicated to us by God, then we may properly regard them as commands issued by one who has the right to be obeyed, and so we may properly use the word 'laws'. In any event, however, such a precept is a hypothetical imperative, telling us what we ought to do if we are to preserve our lives, which of course we all have as our fundamental end. Laws of nature, then, are hypothetical imperatives, prudential obligations. In *De Cive*, Hobbes calls such obligation 'natural obligation'.

I should say at this point that there is dispute among scholars about the interpretation of Hobbes's theory of obligation. What I shall give is my own interpretation, with the warning that it is my own. Hobbes holds that there are two kinds of obligation. (In *De Cive* he writes also of a third kind, physical obligation, but this is not relevant to our purpose.) One is natural obligation, and this is a hypothetical imperative. The other I call artificial obligation, and I regard this as Hobbes's account of what Immanuel Kant was later to call the categorical imperative. Hobbes himself does not anywhere use the expression 'artificial obligation', but he explicitly applies the adjective 'artificial' to covenants or promises (in Chapter 17 of *Leviathan*), and he describes civil laws as 'artificial chains' or 'bonds' (Chapter 21). According to my interpretation of Hobbes, an artificial obligation is a *verbal* obligation or bond, made by a covenant (a promise in consideration of a benefit). In Chapter 15 of *De Cive*, Hobbes contrasts this kind of obligation with natural obligation; and in all three statements of his political theory (*De Corpore Politico*, *De Cive*, and *Leviathan*), he brings out the linguistic character of the obligation of promises. If a man acts contrary to his promise, says Hobbes, he has in effect contradicted himself: for in promising, he has expressed in words a will to do what he promises; and then when he acts in breach of his promise, he wills an action which negates the will he formerly expressed in words. Promise-breaking, therefore, is a kind of self-contradiction, a breach of obligation that is irrational, not in the sense that it is imprudent but in the sense that it is illogical.

To go against a law of nature is irrational in the sense of being imprudent. It is irrational in that it goes against a conclusion of prudential reasoning. To break a promise is not in itself imprudent, though it happens (often, but not always) to be imprudent as well, since it is usually in a man's interest to keep his promises; and therefore one of the laws of nature tells us to keep our promises, provided we can do so without giving a hostage to fortune, but this is an additional consideration to the obligation of the promise itself. In itself, promise-breaking is not imprudent. It is sometimes to a man's advantage to break a promise, and in that case we cannot say that he is 'naturally' or hypothetically obliged to keep his promise. But he still has an artificial or verbal obligation to keep his promise, because it would be illogical or self-contradictory to break it. This artificial obligation has nothing to do with means to an end. The obligation depends entirely on the fact that one has promised. That is why I say that this represents Hobbes's version of what was later to be called the categorical imperative. To break a promise is wrong in itself, just because the promise has been made, not because of any end to which the action of keeping the promise is a means.

Since Hobbes gives the name of natural obligation to hypothetical imperatives, we may say that, for him, the obligation to keep a promise is, in a sense, 'non-natural'. But this does not imply that for Hobbes, as for Kant, there is a world of non-natural entities transcending the world of nature. Hobbes is an ethical naturalist. He is bound to be, since he is also a materialist. He explains ethics in terms of human nature, in terms of psychology. He has a form of non-natural obligation that does not imply anything *super*natural. Non-natural obligation is man-made; it is artificial.

What sort of thing is it? It is simply a contrivance of *language*. According to Hobbes, a natural obligation is a real motive force. A man who is naturally obliged is a man who is moved by fear or hope, by a real psychological force. This natural obligation, a real force, is simulated by that artificial 'obligation' of which we speak when a promise has been made. A man who makes a promise is said to 'bind' himself, by the words he utters, to the performance of an action. But the 'bond' is merely verbal or metaphorical. It is not a bond with any real force. As Hobbes says in *Leviathan*, Chapter 14, 'nothing is more easily broken than a man's word'; and again he says, in Chapter 18, that covenants or promises are 'but words, and breath,' that 'have no force to oblige, contain, constrain, or protect any man, but what it has from the public sword'. (In this quotation, 'oblige' means 'motivate'.) If a promise is to have a real force, to oblige in the sense in which natural obligations oblige, to have a strong motivating power, it must be backed by 'the sword', by physical force that will cause a man to be afraid and to act from his fear. Nevertheless, there is this other kind of obligation that we talk about, and it also comes into Hobbes's theory.

If Hobbes is to persuade men to submit themselves to government, he must show them their *obligation* to do so. As I interpret him, he tells us that we have two kinds of obligation to obey the government. One is the prudential or natural obligation that results from our fear of the effects of anarchy. The other is the non-prudential or artificial obligation of promise-keeping. For Hobbes argues that any citizen of a State may be presumed to have promised obedience. This presumption is set out in Hobbes's theory of a social contract. Hobbes does not, however, suppose that States are normally set up by means of an explicit social contract. He speaks of two methods whereby a commonwealth can be set up, one being social contract, the other conquest; and Hobbes knows very well that most States come into existence by the second method. But he argues that, where a State has been set up by conquest, the subjects can be assumed to have given a tacit promise to obey the ruler in return for having their lives spared. This means that the subject has a double obligation to obey, the first being a prudential obligation depending on his fear of losing his life, the second being the artificial obligation to keep his promise. The point of the social contract theory in Hobbes is to bring out the logical implications of sovereignty and subjection, not to give a fanciful picture of how States may arise by agreement.

Let us now consider in more detail how Hobbes's theory of obligation fits into his political theory. For this purpose we must go back to the idea of laws of nature. When men find themselves in the state of war, their reason prescribes the first law of nature, to seek peace. How are they to do this? By setting up a sovereign authority to lay down laws prescribing what they are required to do and what they may not do. These laws are laws in the ordinary sense of the word, civil laws, not natural laws. Now if a law says that I *must* do X (even if I don't want to) or that I *may not* do Y (even though I want to), this means that it curtails my natural right or liberty to do as I please. There are two *possible* ways of setting up a sovereign authority empowered to do this. One method is by social contract; the other is by conquest. Hobbes calls a State set up by social contract a 'commonwealth by institution', and one set up by conquest he calls a 'commonwealth by acquisition'. He deals first with commonwealth by institution and explains this in great detail. This is not because he thinks that States have in practice arisen by institution. He knows perfectly well that most, if not all, States have come into being as the result of conquest. But he deals first, and most elaborately, with commonwealth by institution because this allows him to bring out the logical implications of what it is to be a subject of a State. We should remember that Hobbes's method of procedure is to find possible causes, not necessarily actual causes. He is going to argue, however, that the logical position is exactly the same irrespective of whether a State has arisen by contract or by conquest. He begins with instituted commonwealth because it happens to be easier to see the logical position in the case of contract and then to observe that the same thing applies to a State set up by conquest.

We can now turn our attention to the second law of nature. How precisely can men get out of the state of war, how can they seek peace? This would be possible if they restrained their desire for power and did not interfere with each other, i.e. if each man restricted his natural right to do as he pleased. Of course this will work only if *everyone* is willing to give up his natural right. The second law of nature therefore states that one should be willing to give up one's natural right to all things so long as other men are willing to do the same. Men can do this by making covenants, which will lay them under obligation (this is artificial obligation) not to attack each other. The obligation restricts their liberty, their right to do as they please. The covenants that they make will be mutually dependent on each other, i.e. they will form a contract. A contract between two or more people consists of mutual promises dependent on each other. Suppose, for example, that I sign a contract with a publisher – or, since we are *imagining*, let us say I sign a contract with a film producer. He promises to pay me a million dollars to act the part of Bottom the Weaver in his production of *A Midsummer Night's Dream*, and I on my side promise to play the part and also promise not to accept any other offer, however tempting, from rival organizations green with envy because they cannot get me to play the ass in *their* productions. Each of us makes his promise on condition that the other party fulfils his promise. And that is a contract – an imaginary one, anyway, which is what we are talking about.

Now in my imaginary case, if one party does not fulfil his side of the bargain, the other party can sue him in a court of law. The law of the State will enforce the contract. But in a state of nature there is no assurance that other people will keep their promises. Promises are but words and breath, they are not real bonds. Nothing is more easily broken than a man's word. Promises are of course useless if they are not kept, and so the third law of nature prescribes that we ought to perform what we promise. According to my interpretation, this 'natural obligation' to keep promises is additional to, and different from, the artificial or verbal obligation that is set up by the promise itself. Prudential reasoning tells us that it will be to our interest to keep our promises. But although this piece of prudential reasoning provides a real motive for action, the precept is not likely to be generally followed unless it is backed by force. It is a prescription of reason, and a purely or mainly rational being would follow it; but men are not purely or mainly rational. Although they can understand what would be the wise or prudent thing to do, their actions are chiefly motivated by passion. Consequently one cannot rely on another man to keep his part of a bargain unless his passions are involved, and this can be brought about by working on his fear. He has to be made afraid of the consequences of breaking his promise. So the proposed system of mutual covenants must be backed by sanctions, by force. The way to do this is for the proposed system of mutual covenants to include the granting of sovereign authority to a common power. What is needed is a social contract in which people covenant together, not just to refrain from exercising their natural rights, but also to set up a common power that will *force* them to refrain from exercising those rights.

Accordingly we can imagine people contracting together in some such terms as follows. Each man promises to give up his natural right to do as he pleases and to act only as he is commanded or allowed by a specified person or assembly of persons, subject to the condition that every other man promises the same thing. Such a contract is giving *authority* to the man (or assembly of men) who is made the *sovereign*. For it is a promise to do what he requires; it is making him the 'author' of one's future acts. As a party to the contract I promise that whatsoever the sovereign wills shall be my will; I submit my will to his. This act of covenanting or promising makes me his *subject*; by giving him authority over me, I lay myself under obligation to obey his commands, i.e. to obey the civil laws.

The social contract, as Hobbes depicts it, is a contract made by all the future citizens of the State with each other. They each promise to give up their natural rights and to obey the person or assembly who is constituted the sovereign of the State. The sovereign himself is not a party to the contract. That is to say, the sovereign makes no promises. Since he is to have absolute authority, his rights must not be limited by any contractual obligation. The sovereign is subject to the laws of nature, as is any man independently of the social contract; but this means that the duties of the sovereign are hypothetical or prudential. It is his duty to keep the peace and to do all things that are necessary to maintain security; this is because a failure to do so will mean a reversion to the state of war, which he does not want any more than others do. The sovereign has no contractual or artificial obligations; he is not a party to the contract, he makes no promises. He therefore retains the full measure of natural right, he is at liberty to do whatever he thinks fit. The subjects are obliged by the contract to obey the laws that the sovereign enacts. But the sovereign himself is above the laws of the State. He has not promised to abide by them. In this sense the king can do no wrong. He cannot act unjustly, for injustice, according to Hobbes, is breach of covenant, and the sovereign has made no covenant. One of the laws of nature prescribes equity, i.e. equal or impartial dealing between men if one has to judge them. The sovereign has a natural or prudential obligation to follow this law of nature like others, and a king who is partial in judgement acts inequitably. Hobbes distinguishes, however, between equity and justice; justice is the keeping of covenant and injustice is the breach of covenant, and since the sovereign has not covenanted to obey the civil laws, as his subjects have, he cannot be said to break those laws or thereby to act unjustly. He has absolute right and therefore absolute authority.

Corresponding to the absolute authority of the sovereign, the subject has an almost absolute obligation of obedience. The obligation of the subject is almost absolute but not quite. There are some things which a subject is not obliged to do. These are described in Chapter 21 of *Leviathan*. A man has 'liberty to disobey' if the sovereign orders him 'to kill, wound, or maim himself; or not to resist those that assault him; or to abstain from the use of food, air, medicine, or any other thing without which he cannot live'. If he is commanded to fight as a soldier, 'though his sovereign have right enough to punish his refusal with death', he 'may nevertheless in many cases refuse, without injustice; as when he substituteth a sufficient soldier in his place'. Other liberties 'depend on the silence of the law'. But the whole obligation of subjects to the sovereign lasts only as long as the power which the sovereign has to protect them. 'The end of obedience is protection.' The reason for the limitations upon the obligation of subjects is this. The subjects have entered into the social contract in order to preserve their lives. They cannot therefore be presumed to have promised to do anything which will go against that ultimate aim. Nevertheless the sovereign is perfectly entitled to issue a command that a subject should kill himself or should not resist those who come to arrest him; and if the subject refuses to obey this command, as he on his side is entitled to do, then the sovereign may order him to be punished by death.

I have already said that Hobbes is well aware that in practice States are unlikely to be set up by social contract. A State is usually set up by the alternative method of conquest. But, Hobbes points out, the result-ant position is exactly the same. The sovereign has absolute authority, and the subject has an almost absolute obligation. Furthermore, the subject's obligation is of the same kind as in an instituted common-wealth, that is to say, it includes the artificial obligation of covenant or promising. When the victor in a battle has the vanquished in his power, he is in a position to do just what he likes with them; we might picture him as being able to stand over each vanquished person with a drawn sword, in a position to kill him. Now Hobbes holds that if the victor does not kill the vanquished, we may *presume* that the vanquished implicitly promises to do whatever the victor orders him to do, so long as his life is spared. By such an implicit promise of obedience the vanquished becomes the *subject* of the conqueror. In this instance the subject makes his promise directly to the sovereign, as contrasted with commonwealth by institution where the future subjects make promises to each other. But in this instance as much as in the former one, the sovereign makes no promises and therefore has no artificial obligations. In the case of commonwealth by acquisition there is no contract (i.e. a set of mutual covenants); instead there is simply a series of covenants made from one side only. The subject promises to obey so long as his life is spared; but the sovereign does not promise to spare the subject's life. The sovereign still has the right, which he had at the beginning, to take the subject's life if he chooses to do so; his right remains absolute. But the sovereign can count on the subject's obedience only so long as he does not exercise his right to take the subject's life, for the subject's promise to obey is given with that limitation. Consequently, in an acquired commonwealth as in an instituted commonwealth, if the sub-ject is ordered to do something which will endanger his life, he is not obliged to obey. We can see, then, that the main point of the earlier account of a social contract, or of a commonwealth by institution, is simply to bring out clearly the logical implications of sovereignty and subjection, namely, the fact that the sovereign has an absolute right, while the subject has an almost absolute obligation of obedience, de-pending upon an assumed promise.

But, one may ask, why should Hobbes want to talk at all about an assumed promise in the case of a State that arises by conquest? Since the conqueror has the vanquished in his power, what need is there to speak of the obligation of a supposed promise? The subject will have a natural obligation to obey, just as a man is naturally obliged to hand over his money to a thug who points a revolver at him and says 'Your money or your life'. Hobbes is not satisfied with this, however. In Chapter 20 of *Leviathan*, he draws a distinction between a subject or a servant on the one hand, and a captive or a slave on the other. A captive or a slave is in the power of his master, but he has no obligation other than natural obligation. If he can manage to run away, he is not obliged to refrain from doing so. By contrast, a subject or a servant has an obligation *towards* his master (not just the natural obligation to do the best he can for himself). The master has not merely power over him, but also authority, i.e. a right to be obeyed. And if the subject or servant has an obligation *towards* his master, that kind of obligation must be based on a promise.

The point of the distinction is this. The obligations of promises, if not backed by power, are merely verbal and have little force to act as a motive. But on the other hand, power by itself is not adequate either. Of course, the exercise of power goes a long way in getting people to obey their masters' will. A captive or a slave simply has to do as he is told, for the most part. But a State cannot be run on the lines of a prison. When the conqueror has the vanquished actually before him at the point of the sword, he can rely on the threat of force to get his wishes carried out. But he cannot be in this position all the time. When he is not on the spot, the other man may run away, just as a captive may run away if he is not kept locked up. Therefore something else besides the exercise of power is required for running a State. This something else is acknowledged authority, whereby the sovereign has a *right* to be obeyed, and the subjects have an *obligation to him* to obey. In order to provide for this, Hobbes brings in the idea of a supposed covenant.

We now see the purpose of the social contract theory in Hobbes, and we can also see why he makes political obligation a combination of two kinds of obligation, natural and artificial. A man ought to obey the laws of the State for two reasons. The first reason is that it is in his interest to obey, i.e. he has a natural obligation; the State is intended to avoid the natural state of war, and however irksome the laws of the State may be, anything (save the instant threat of death) is better than the condition of war or anarchy, in which life is nasty, brutish, and short. Secondly, there is also an artificial obligation, depending upon a presumed promise to obey; the presumption is necessary for the relations of sovereignty and subjection, without which a State cannot work.

This, then, is Hobbes's political theory, his justification of political obedience. It has been carried out in accordance with his prescribed method, seeking relations of cause and effect, for the purpose of being useful to the life of man. In the course of explaining his political theory, Hobbes has given us a moral theory, a theory of the nature of man, of good and evil, and especially a theory of obligations and rights. Hobbes's analysis of two kinds of obligation allows for a distinction between hypothetical and non-hypothetical obligations, and yet the whole theory remains naturalistic, that is to say, a theory which depends entirely upon the data of experience and makes no presuppositions about transcendental values or norms.

Chapter V

Morals and Politics – II

Having given a general outline of Hobbes's theory of morals and politics, I want now to discuss in some detail certain points of particular philosophical interest. I shall pick out for comment a number of passages in the text of *Leviathan*.

First, I take Hobbes's account of the psychology of action in Chapter 6. Hobbes begins by distinguishing between 'vital motion' and 'animal or voluntary motion'. By vital motion Hobbes means physiological motion, and he says that it takes place without any 'help of imagination', while animal or voluntary motion is to do something 'as is first fancied in our minds'. This means that vital motion takes place without consciousness, while animal or voluntary motion is conscious behaviour. According to Hobbes, imagination or fancy is the mental appearance of physiological motion, and this precedes the animal motion. The particular kind of 'fancy' (i.e. consciousness) which precedes action is the 'small beginnings' of animal motion, and is called 'endeavour'. Of this there are two species, appetite or desire, and aversion; the first being motion towards a thing, the second being motion away from a thing. Hobbes notes that the Latin words from which 'appetite' and 'aversion' are derived, and likewise one pair of Greek equivalents, have as their basic meaning a literal movement towards or away from an object.

Hobbes next proceeds to define love and hate in terms of desire and aversion. He says that love and desire are identical except that we commonly speak of love when the object of our appetite is present, and of desire when the object is absent. Similarly hate and aversion are identical except that the use of the word 'hate' usually implies that the object is present while the use of the word 'aversion' implies that the object is absent. This distinction leads one to ask just how desire and aversion are to be regarded as forms of motion. In the case of love and hate, since the object of our feeling is present it makes sense to speak of moving towards or away from that object; but in the case of desire and aversion the object is supposed to be absent, and in that event how can one speak of moving towards it or away from it? I suppose Hobbes would say that when we have a desire we move in a direction which we think is likely to bring us into the presence of the object. For example, when Colonel Chinstrap wants a tot of whisky and finds that there is none in the house, he goes along to the local pub, where he thinks whisky is to be found. Hobbes would say that Chinstrap's desire for a tot is the internal beginning of movement out of his house towards the place where he thinks he will find whisky. On the other hand, if Chinstrap is standing at the bar of the pub, drinking whisky, and feels that he wants to go on drinking whisky, he might describe his feelings by saying that he loves the stuff.

Hobbes then proceeds in this chapter to give definitions of the terms 'good' and 'evil'. They are defined as the *object* of desire and of aversion respectively. If I call a thing good, according to Hobbes this means that I want it; and if I call a thing bad, this means that I dislike it. The words 'good' and 'evil', Hobbes says, 'are ever used with relation to the person that useth them: there being nothing simply and absolutely so'. Hobbes denies that there is any absolute sense of good. The idea that a thing is good is always relative to the desires of someone. We can, however, speak of something as being good or bad for all; in Hobbes's words, we can have a 'common rule of good and evil'; but then this common rule is relative to a *decision* by a ruler, judge, or arbitrator. For instance, it is perfectly possible for me to say 'Hitting people on the nose is bad' even though I myself may have no aversion from hitting people on the nose; but in this case my criterion is the rule set up by the law which forbids assault and battery, or else it is the dictum of the judge in court who admonishes me by saying (though in more forceful language) 'Hitting people on the nose is very bad'. The rule of the law, or the admonition of the judge, is the expression of a command or injunction, and according to Hobbes a command is the expression of a desire. So if one says that assault and battery are bad, even though the speaker quite likes going round assaulting people, what he means, in Hobbes's view, is that the State forbids it.

Having defined the notions of good and evil in terms of desire and aversion, Hobbes then considers pleasure and displeasure. These he regards as the mental appearances of good and evil. Objects of desire, when attained, help vital motion and so give pleasure. When we attain an object of desire, i.e. a good, we feel pleasure; so pleasure is the appearance, the felt awareness, of good. Conversely the object of aversion, if it comes to us despite our attempt to avoid it, causes displeasure; so that displeasure is the mental appearance of evil, i.e. of the object of aversion.

Following up these definitions of love, hate, good, evil, pleasure, and displeasure, in terms of his original concept of endeavour (appetite and aversion), Hobbes proceeds to give a long list of further definitions of psychological terms built up likewise from the notions of appetite and aversion or else from notions that in their turn depend on these. Certain items in this list are worthy of note for different reasons. I take first his definitions of *benevolence* and *pity* because these were subjected to well-known and important criticisms by Bishop Butler in his *Fifteen Sermons preached at the Rolls Chapel* (published in 1726).

In Chapter 6 of *Leviathan*, Hobbes treats as synonymous the terms 'benevolence', 'good will', and 'charity', and he defines them as simply 'desire of good to another'. When we recall that Hobbes has defined 'good' as the object of desire, we see that his definition of benevolence comes to saying that it is desiring for another person what he desires for himself. This seems an unexceptionable definition. But it is customary to say that Hobbes's account of benevolence is paradoxically egoistic and that the falsity of an egoistic psychology is shown by Bishop Butler's criticism of Hobbes's definitions of benevolence and of pity. Butler in fact refers, not to *Leviathan*, but to Hobbes's fuller account of psychology in *Human Nature*. In Chapter 9 of that work, Hobbes says this:

> There is yet another passion sometimes called love, but more properly good will or charity. There can be no greater argument to a man, of his own power, than to find himself able not only to accomplish his own desires, but also to assist other men in theirs: and this is that conception wherein consisteth charity.

Butler, in a long footnote to Sermon 1, takes Hobbes to be here *defining* good will or charity as a delight in the exercise of power to help others. I do not think Hobbes is in fact doing this. It seems to me that he *defines* good will or charity simply as helping others; but he implies that the *reason why* men display benevolence or good will is that they obtain pleasure from the exercise of their power in doing so. However that may be in *Human Nature*, it is perfectly clear that the definition of benevolence or good will or charity in *Leviathan* is straightforward and satisfactory, the desire of good to another.

The same can be said of Hobbes's definition of pity a little later in Chapter 6 of *Leviathan*. He defines pity as 'grief for the calamity of another', which is unexceptionable; but he goes on to give an egoistic account of the *cause* of pity. Pity arises, Hobbes says, from the imagination that the like calamity may befall oneself. In *Human Nature*, however, Hobbes says that pity *is* 'imagination or fiction of future calamity to ourselves, proceeding from the sense of another man's calamity', and Butler criticizes this. Hobbes's definition of pity in *Human Nature* certainly is egoistic and is properly a target for Butler's criticism. It is worth noting, incidentally, that Hobbes's account of pity is derived from Aristotle's *Rhetoric*. Aristotle's egoistic conception, in the *Rhetoric*, of pity as a form of fear explains why Aristotle couples pity and fear together in his account of the tragic emotions in the *Poetics*.

While Butler's criticism of Hobbes on benevolence is off the mark because Hobbes does not in fact *define* benevolence egoistically, nevertheless Butler's criticisms of Hobbes both on benevolence and on pity are worth attention as examples of careful philosophical criticism. The comment on benevolence comes in a footnote to Sermon 1, and that on pity in a footnote to Sermon 5.

On benevolence Butler argues as follows. If benevolence were the same as delight in the exercise of power, then it would be impossible to have the one without the other. But in fact this is possible. A man may wish to help another, although not able to do so, and he may be pleased to find a third person, who is able to render the help, doing so. Here the first man does not have the *power* to help, but nevertheless feels benevolence or good will. It is therefore possible for benevolence to exist without delight in the exercise of power. Conversely there can be delight in the exercise of power without there being benevolence, and this would be impossible if the two things were identical. Butler points out that if a man displays cruelty to another, he is exercising power, and it is possible for him to take pleasure in it (this is what sadism consists in). Now cruelty is the opposite of benevolence, but according to Hobbes's definition (as Butler understands it) there would be no difference between benevolence and cruelty. In fact, as I have said before, Hobbes does not maintain that benevolence *is* delight in the exercise of power; but he does seem to think that delight in the exercise of power is the only reason a man can have for being benevolent; and the first half of Butler's criticism shows that this is mistaken. A man can feel benevolence even though he does not have the power to put it into effect.

On pity Butler argues that if pity is the imagination of calamity to ourselves, then it follows that pity is the same thing as fear, which is obviously absurd. This identification would imply, among other things, that fear or cowardice is a virtue, since pity or compassion is a virtue. Hobbes's definition of pity in *Leviathan*, however, does not state that pity is the same as fear for ourselves but only that it arises from the thought that we ourselves may fall into a similar calamity. This is still an implausible view but it does not have the particular implications that Butler points out and that can be said to fault the account in *Human Nature*.

Next we should note Hobbes's definitions of *deliberation* and *will*. Deliberation, according to Hobbes, is simply the succession of different forms of appetite and aversion. Hobbes assumes that the Latin word *delibero* means putting an end to liberty. It does not make sense to deliberate about what is impossible or about what is past and done with. One can deliberate only when one has a choice, a freedom, of acting according to one's desires. And since deliberation ends with a decision and an action, it puts an end to the liberty, it makes the act one that is done and so no longer a mere possibility.

Hobbes's etymology here is mistaken. The word *delibero* has to do with weighing (from *libra*, a balance), and not with the idea of *liber*, free. In any case, Hobbes's fanciful derivation does not fit his account, for it is *willing*, not deliberation, that puts an end to the open possibilities. So long as we deliberate, it is still open to us to go one way or the other.

The will, according to Hobbes, is simply the last appetite or aversion in deliberation. Owing to his materialist account of endeavour, Hobbes assumes that the cause of action (animal motion) must be the internal motion of endeavour. So he says that willing an action is just desiring to do it; but it is distinguished from the other desires that have come up in the process of deliberation, simply because it is the last one and so is the directly effective cause of the action. Hobbes is influenced by the derivation of 'will' from roots meaning 'wish' and by the fact that the Latin *voluntas* does duty for both. We speak of doing a thing 'willingly' when we mean simply 'according to our wishes' or 'not against our wishes'. And again he is influenced by the use of the word 'will' to describe a person's written expression of his wishes before he dies, and especially of the phrase 'the last will and testament of . . .'. In *Human Nature* Hobbes says that the expressions 'will' and 'last will' mean the same thing, namely, the last wish or desire before effective action.

Because all animal motion is preceded by endeavour, whether or not this endeavour occurs as the last of a series, it follows that all animal motion is of the same kind, being caused by a desire of which we are conscious. Therefore, in Hobbes's view, we may say in every case that it is 'willed' and so is *voluntary* motion, unlike physiological movements ('vital motion') which are not caused by an endeavour of which we are conscious.

Towards the end of Chapter 6, Hobbes defines *felicity*, i.e. happiness. It is, he says, continual success in obtaining the things which a man desires from time to time. Hobbes denies the view that perfect happiness, in this life at least, could be a calm or tranquil state, such as the happiness of heaven is supposed to be. If a man were altogether at rest, he would indeed be out of this world, he would be dead. 'For there is no such thing as perpetual tranquillity of mind, while we live here; because life itself is but motion, and can never be without desire, nor without fear, no more than without sense.' This conception of felicity or happiness affects Hobbes's political theory too, and comes up again in Chapter 11.

Before leaving these comments on points of detail in Chapter 6, it is worth noting three definitions that do not directly affect Hobbes's theory of morals and politics but which nevertheless are of interest to a student of his philosophy. These are his definitions of *curiosity*, *religion*, and *laughter*.

Hobbes defines curiosity as the desire to know why and how. There is nothing remarkable about this simple definition. What is interesting is that Hobbes adds the comment that curiosity exists in no living creatures other than man, so that curiosity as well as reason are what distinguish man from other animals. He is of course thinking of the traditional Aristotelian definition of man as a rational animal, and Hobbes's addition of curiosity, the desire to know why and how, as a further *differentia* between man and other animals illustrates the value that Hobbes sets upon science, the finding out of causes.

Hobbes defines religion as the fear of invisible power, and he distinguishes it from superstition simply by saying that the fear is called religion if the stories of invisible power are publicly allowed, and superstition if they are not. I am reminded of a remark that Bertrand Russell once made in a television appearance with a group of Asiatic students. He was asked if he thought that prejudice on issues of morals and politics was sometimes due to religious belief, and he replied that he did. The chairman of the discussion then asked if it was not superstition rather than religion which had these bad effects, and Russell rejoined in his dry way: 'I don't understand the distinction you are making.' Hobbes, however, does write also, in his definition, of 'true religion', which is religion when the invisible power imagined is truly such as we imagine. I suppose Hobbes is implying that the common conceptions of religion are religion (because publicly allowed) but not true; while his own idea of God is true, namely, that God is the cause of the world, absolutely powerful, but beyond that unknown to us.

Hobbes also gives in this chapter a brief statement of his theory of laughter as 'sudden glory', i.e. sudden pleasure in the thought (true or false) of one's own power. On this view, we laugh (if we do) at the man who slips on a banana skin because we are pleased to find that we are superior to him, while the victim himself does not laugh because he feels inferior. This is one of the two or three main theories of laughter, and Hobbes was the first to put it forward. In *Human Nature* he gives a fuller account and begins by saying that no one has previously produced any satisfactory explanation of laughter. Hobbes's theory does not account for all laughter, e.g. laughter at sheer incongruity, as in verbal

wit, or the laughter of a child from sheer happiness. Not many philosophers, even among those who are interested in Aesthetics, have reflected to any purpose on the comic and laughter. Hobbes will have been
interested in the subject no doubt because he himself was a master of a
certain kind of wit, and while his theory is too narrow it is certainly
fitted rather cleverly into his general psychology.

From Chapter 6 of *Leviathan* I turn to Chapter 10, which begins with
the notion of *power*. Hobbes defines the power of a man as his present
means to obtain some future apparent good. We need to remember that
'apparent good' means pleasure, because pleasure was defined in Chapter
6 as the appearance or sense of good. The definition of power therefore
comes to saying that power is the means to obtain future pleasure.
Hobbes illustrates different kinds of power and says that the greatest of
human powers is political power, being a combination of the powers of
most men in a sovereign.

Having illustrated different kinds of power, Hobbes goes on to define
the *value* or *worth* of a man.

> The *value*, or WORTH of a man, is as of all other things, his price; that
> is to say, so much as would be given for the use of his power: and
> therefore is not absolute; but a thing dependent on the need and
> judgement of another. . . . And as in other things, so in men, not the
> seller, but the buyer determines the price.

It will be remembered that Hobbes defined the term 'good', applied to a
thing, as the object of desire, with the consequence that it was relative,
not absolute. He now defines the value of a person in terms of his
power. Power is an object of desire, and therefore good or valuable. If a
man has power, that power is esteemed as valuable. The amount of
value set upon a thing or a person is to be estimated, according to
Hobbes, in economic terms of price; it depends on what other people
would be prepared to give for it or for the use of it. Diamonds are
valued, they are an object of desire. The amount of value to be set upon
them as compared with other things depends on what people are prepared to pay; that is, what other desirable things they are prepared to
give up in exchange for the diamonds. A man who is prepared to pay
£100 for a diamond is giving up the means of obtaining other desirable
things which his money could otherwise purchase. Likewise, if I am
prepared to hire a labourer for £50 a week, this means that I set a
certain value on the use of his physical power. And if I am prepared to
pay similarly for the services of a doctor, this means that I set a certain
value on the use of his ability, his power, to cure me of my illness.

It is of course undoubtedly true that we do set a value upon men in

47

economic terms after this fashion. We set a greater value upon the services of a doctor than upon the services of a gardener. What is peculiar about Hobbes's view is that he implies this is the *only* natural way of valuing men. That is to say, Hobbes holds that the conception of a good man is, in purely natural terms, no different from the conception of a good doctor or a good gardener. (Plato took the same view, comparing the goodness or virtue of a man with the functional value of a thing or animal, as when we speak of a good knife or a good sheepdog.) If you are picking a football team, you may say 'Brown is a good man', meaning that he has good ability as a footballer. Now Hobbes refers to *this* kind of human value at the end of the chapter, where he distinguishes worth from *worthiness*. Worthiness refers to a particular ability or aptitude, while worth refers to power or ability in general. So that, according to Hobbes, to say of someone that he is a good man, without referring to a particular ability, is simply to say that he is a powerful individual, someone whom you esteem for his power.

Such esteeming is *honour*. A man is honoured for his power, and Hobbes defines *honourable* as 'whatsoever possession, action, or quality, is an argument and sign of power'. A little later he says: 'Dominion, and victory is honourable; because acquired by power; and servitude, for need, or fear, is dishonourable.' He also says this: 'Nor does it alter the case of honour, whether an action (so it be great and difficult, and consequently a sign of much power,) be just or unjust: for honour consisteth only in the opinion of power.'

It is important to be clear that Hobbes is here giving a description of what he takes to be the *natural* type of valuation and esteem. Hobbes is not himself recommending that we should honour an action if it is a sign of power, even though it is unjust. He is saying that this is what naturally happens. According to Hobbes, as we shall see later, *justice* and *injustice* have to do with *artificial* morality, that is to say with the keeping or breaking of promises. Hobbes himself wants to recommend to us this artificial kind of morality, not the natural morality of honour. He takes the code of honour to be the natural type of morality and to be in fact bad since it leads to the state of war. Men naturally desire power and esteem power, but this leads to the undesirable state of war. In the next paragraph of Chapter 10, Hobbes speaks of the moral code of people before the time when there were 'great commonwealths'.

[It was then] thought no dishonour to be a pirate, or a highway thief; but rather a lawful trade, not only amongst the Greeks, but also amongst all other nations; as is manifest by the histories of ancient time. And at this day, in this part of the world, private duels are, and always will be honourable, though unlawful, till such time as there shall be honour ordained for them that refuse, and ignominy for them that make the challenge.

Hobbes himself does not approve of regarding piracy and duelling as honourable. He would prefer to see duelling dishonourable and the refusal to take part counted as honourable. Hobbes himself is against the old code of honour. But his point is that this is the way men naturally behave; this code represents the valuations that they naturally take. To replace this code of honour by the code of justice requires the artificial organization of the State.

In Chapter 11 Hobbes returns to the idea of felicity, continuing what he has said in Chapter 6. The tradition of Greek philosophy had spoken of happiness as man's highest end or good. Hobbes rejects this conception.

> For there is no such *finis ultimus*, (utmost aim,) nor *summum bonum*, (greatest good,) as is spoken of in the books of the old moral philosophers. Nor can a man any more live, whose desires are at an end, than he, whose senses and imaginations are at a stand [because, as we remember from Chapter 6, life itself is but motion]. Felicity [i.e. happiness] is a continual progress of the desire, from one object to another ... The cause whereof is, that the object of man's desire, is not to enjoy once only, and for one instant of time; but to assure for ever, the way of his future desire. ...
> So that in the first place, I put for a general inclination of all mankind, a perpetual and restless desire of power after power, that ceaseth only in death.

The reason why the desire for power never ceases is that men want to be assured of maintaining in the future their present level of power and pleasure, and so they continually seek more power. Hobbes goes on to say that competition for power leads to contention and war, and this thought is further developed in Chapter 13.

Chapter 13 describes 'the natural condition of mankind', the state of war. Hobbes begins with the natural equality of men, not an equality of rights or of worth but an equality of ability, which leads to equality of hope in attaining one's ends and so to competition. After defining and describing the state of war, in which life is 'solitary, poor, nasty, brutish, and short', Hobbes adds some apt empirical evidence for the conclusion which he appears to have reached purely by abstract reasoning from a conception of human psychology. It may seem strange to some, says Hobbes, that nature should make men hostile to one another, but the conclusion reached by reasoning from the definitions of the natural passions can be confirmed by experience. Even in an organized society, with its system of security, human behaviour shows distrust. Men lock their doors and their chests even though they know there is a law and a police force to punish injuries. How much more must one expect distrust in a situation where there is no organized system of protection ?

Hobbes ends these remarks by emphasizing that to find the cause of strife in human nature is not to accuse human nature. Natural desires and passions, he says, 'are in themselves no sin'. Nor are the actions that are motivated by these passions, unless there is a law that forbids certain actions. In the state of nature there is no question of 'sin', i.e. of wrongdoing. There is no question of right action or wrong action before men have any conception of laws that lay obligations upon them.

Hobbes agrees that his picture of a primitive state of war may be unhistorical. He explicitly says that he does not believe it ever generally existed for mankind as a whole, though it does apply to some savage tribes, such as the American Indians, who do not have any system of government except in small families, where order depends, in Hobbes's view, upon the sexual instincts. Nevertheless the natural state which he has described is that into which a society tends to degenerate, in the form of civil war, if the sovereignty of the government is not maintained. Then again, Hobbes says, the state of war is well illustrated in the relations *between* States, because there is no supra-national authority.

'To this war of every man against every man, this also is consequent; that nothing can be unjust. The notions of right and wrong, justice and injustice have there no place. Where there is no common power, there is no law: where no law, no injustice.' Justice and injustice do not apply to the individual alone, they relate to society. Consequently also, in the natural state, there is no conception of property, of mine and thine. Every man is free to take what he can.

The motives for getting out of the state of war are fear of death, desire of things useful for a more comfortable life, and the hope of obtaining these by industry. Of these motives, the fear of death is first and fundamental. Because of the desire men have to remove themselves from the state of war, reason suggests 'articles of peace', the laws of nature.

The laws of nature are described in Chapters 14 and 15. Chapter 14 begins, however, by defining the *right of nature*, which Hobbes firmly distinguishes from the idea of a law of nature.

The RIGHT OF NATURE, which writers commonly call *jus naturale*, is the liberty each man hath, to use his own power, as he will himself, for the preservation of his own nature; that is to say, of his own life; and consequently, of doing any thing, which in his own judgement, and reason, he shall conceive to be the aptest means thereunto.

Hobbes then defines *liberty* as 'the absence of external impediments'.

There is a difficulty here. If we take strictly the word 'external' in Hobbes's definition of liberty, and if we think of men in the state of nature, it will not be true that a man has a right to all things. For a right to all things means a liberty to do anything, and the definition of liberty should imply that there are no external impediments on a man's doing whatever he likes. But in fact the actions of other men, in competition with his own, are frequently liable to impede his doing what he wants.

Although Hobbes normally means by the word 'liberty' the absence of *any* external impediments, here he wants to mean only a particular class of impediments, namely, the obligations laid on us by laws. He means that in the state of nature a man is free to do whatever he chooses, in the sense that he *may* do whatever he chooses, not in the sense that he *can*. In the state of nature there are no *legal* or *moral* impediments, no obligations requiring him to refrain from certain actions. But it is not the case that there are no *physical* impediments. The distinction between 'may' and 'can' – what I *may* do, what I am legally or morally *entitled* to do; and what I *can* do, what I have the *power* to do – is insufficiently noted by Hobbes, and provides a ground for criticizing his account of liberty.

Hobbes next defines a *law of nature* as 'a precept, or general rule, found out by reason,' which requires us to do what will conduce to self-preservation and to avoid what is destructive of one's life. He distinguishes sharply between right and law, *ius* and *lex*. 'RIGHT, consisteth in liberty to do, or to forbear; whereas LAW, determineth, and bindeth to one of them: so that law, and right, differ as much, as obligation, and liberty; which in one and the same matter are inconsistent.' This illustrates what Hobbes was after when he defined natural right earlier as liberty. Natural right is a freedom from obligation. Obligation is a restriction of liberty or right.

I want to make two comments here about Hobbes's break with tradition in his use of the terms 'natural law' and 'natural right', *lex naturalis* and *ius naturale*.

(1) The traditional idea of natural law, prominent in medieval moral philosophy, represents a fusion of ideas taken from the Stoics, from Roman jurisprudence, and from biblical theology. According to this traditional view, natural laws or laws of nature are moral laws laid down by God for men to follow in their conduct. These natural laws for man differ from the laws that God has laid down for the rest of the creation. The rest of the creation works necessarily, and the laws of its working are the causal laws that science studies. Man, however, according to the traditional idea, has free will; he can choose either to follow God's law or not to follow it. Natural law tells us how we *ought* to act, the word 'ought' being used in a moral sense. The obligations prescribed by

natural law will include obligations towards others, obligations to our fellowmen and obligations to God.

Hobbes's position is to regard laws of nature as purely prudential (or what Kant was later to call hypothetical) obligations. They are not therefore what we commonly mean by moral obligations; and they are not obligations towards other persons. As I read Hobbes, he thinks of the idea of obligation towards another person as being confined to the class of *artificial* obligations, obligations of covenant. The traditional view of the obligations of natural law employs the concept of obligation in the categorical sense, Hobbes employs it in this context in the hypothetical sense.

(2) In the traditional conception, the whole system of natural obligations could also be called *Ius Naturale*. It is common in legal contexts to call a whole system of law by the name *ius*. Thus we have, in Latin, the *Ius Civile* (the Civil Law), and the *Ius Gentium* (the Law of Nations). Similarly in French today, the expression *le droit* can mean 'the law'; and the same goes for the German use of *Recht* or the Italian *diritto*.

Hobbes thinks it is a mistake to link the notions of law and right, *lex* and *ius*, in this way. He considers that they should be opposed to each other. The reason for this second change in Hobbes is again that he is using the key term in a different sense from that of traditional natural law theory. The noun 'right' has two different senses.

(i) We may speak of having a right *to do* something, e.g. 'I have a right to stand on my head'. To say this is equivalent to saying that I have no obligation to refrain. A right in this sense is a freedom from obligation. To say that a person has a right to do something is to say that he may do it, he is permitted to do it. In order to mark this sense of 'a right' we may call it a 'right of action', or a 'licence' (that which is licit, allowed, not forbidden), or, as Hobbes calls it, a 'liberty'.

(ii) We may speak of having a right *to* something, i.e. a right to receive something from somebody; and therefore it can also be spoken of as a right *against* somebody. To recall the fantastic example of a contract that I used in Chapter 4, I may say that I have a right to the million dollars owed to me by the film producer for playing the part of Bottom the Weaver in the production of *A Midsummer Night's Dream*. It is a right against the film producer, and it is a right to receive the money. To say that I have a right to the money is equivalent to saying that the person against whom I have the right has an obligation to me. If I have a right against the film producer, this means that he owes me the money, he is obliged to pay up. In order to mark this sense of 'a right', we may call it a 'right of recipience' (a right to *receive* something) or a 'due claim' (something *owed* to me). Hobbes says of a claim that the person who has it has it 'as due'.

The traditional conception of natural law referred not only to obligations towards other persons but correspondingly to rights against other persons. If I am obliged to respect the life of another person, it follows that he has the right to receive such respect from me. So a system of obligations in this sense can also be described as a system of rights (dues). But since Hobbes thinks of natural obligation in the sense of hypothetical obligation, a precept of prudence, it is not obligation towards other persons, and therefore it does not have corresponding to it a right of recipience, a due claim, of those other persons. In order to give a meaning to the notion of natural right, therefore, Hobbes uses the other sense of the noun 'right', in which it means a right of action, a licence, or a liberty, a freedom to act with absence of obligation. In this sense, as Hobbes says, a right is opposed to an obligation.

According to Hobbes, a categorical obligation, or an obligation towards another person, and likewise a right of recipience, a right against another person, can only arise from a covenant. This is exemplified in my imaginary right against the film producer, which arose from our contract. Such an obligation and right are artificial. Hobbes tries so far as possible to confine the noun 'right' to the first sense of the term, the one that I have called a right of action, but as he proceeds with his political theory a right of recipience creeps in unawares. When I as a citizen covenant to obey the sovereign, he has a recipient right of obedience; he has a right to receive obedience from me. For this is just another way of saying that I am obliged to obey him, as I have covenanted. In addition, however, the sovereign also has the natural right (the right of action) of doing anything he chooses, since he has not limited his natural right by any covenant. Hobbes's original intention was to hold that the right of the sovereign consists entirely of natural right, i.e. a right of action, but this part of Hobbes's theory unintentionally brings in the concept of a recipient right also.

Having defined and distinguished natural right and natural law, Hobbes recalls that the condition of man in a state of nature is a condition of war, in which every man has a right to everything with the consequence that no one has any security. Accordingly, says Hobbes, it is a precept or general rule of reason that every man ought to seek peace. This is the first law of nature. Hobbes refers to two branches of the 'rule' of reason, (i) to seek peace, and (ii) if we cannot obtain peace, to defend ourselves. Only the first of these two branches is a law of nature; the second branch of this 'rule' gives 'the sum of the right of nature'. This 'second branch', to defend ourselves if we cannot obtain peace, is not a second law of nature. The second law of nature is given later, namely, that a man should be willing to lay down his right to all things if other men are willing to do the same.

Hobbes then goes on to explain how you can lay down a right. To do this is to divest yourself of liberty, i.e. it is to place yourself under an obligation, where before you were free to do as you pleased. Consequently Hobbes adds that when a man lays down a right he is said to be *obliged* or *bound* not to exercise the right which he has abandoned. If he acts against his obligation his action is unjust; he does an injury, since he acts *sine jure*, without right. The idea is that he does what he has no right of action to do. In fact, I think, the etymological meaning of injustice or injury relates to the other meaning of *ius*, a right: injustice or injury is going against a right of recipience held by one or more other persons.

Hobbes then proceeds to compare injustice to logical absurdity, i.e. to self-contradiction. The idea is that a man has first expressed a will, by words or other signs, to renounce his right, and then, in exercising the right nevertheless, he expresses a will to the contrary. The signs whereby a right is renounced are 'the BONDS, by which men are bound, and obliged', bonds which in themselves are weak but may be reinforced by fear of evil consequences.

Continuing to elaborate his conception of transferring or renouncing a right, Hobbes says that such an action is always done in consideration for an advantage to be gained. 'For it is a voluntary act: and of the voluntary acts of every man, the object is some *good to himself*.' The statement that the object of every voluntary act is a good to oneself is a vestige of the egoistic psychology which Hobbes held when he wrote *Human Nature* but which he had generally modified by the time he came to write *Leviathan*. This particular sentence is one of several which show the traces of the earlier psychological egoism. Although Hobbes is not strictly an egoist in the general doctrine of *Leviathan*, his earlier adherence to egoism still infects some of his doctrines and especially his doctrine of covenant, which is of course essential to his political theory. In the present passage of Chapter 14, Hobbes goes on to say that, because the object of a voluntary act is always some good to oneself, certain rights *cannot* be abandoned and notably the right to resistance when one's life is threatened. So if a man uses words that seem to involve a transfer of this right, he is not to be understood as meaning it; we must assume instead that he does not know what he is doing.

Hobbes then goes into details about the different kinds of covenants that can be made, whereby rights are transferred. Among these is *contract*, which is a mutual transferring of right. In the state of nature, Hobbes tells us, there is no security that covenants will be kept. If a man has made a contract in a state of nature, and then later has reason to suspect that the other party will not perform his side of the bargain, then the first man is not bound to keep *his* promise. But such fear or suspicion will not be reasonable in a commonwealth, where the executive power of the government provides security that the performance of promises will be enforced.

Hobbes also says in this part of Chapter 14 that covenants which are made from fear in the first instance are valid and obligatory. To act from fear is to act voluntarily. Hobbes's doctrine here is out of line with the tradition of jurisprudence, which holds that a covenant made under duress is void. The reason why Hobbes insists on his unusual point of view is that he wants to argue later, in Chapter 20, that a tacit covenant made with a conqueror is not invalid merely because the motive for making it was fear of suffering something worse in the first place. When Hobbes spoke earlier of a covenant being made invalid by fear of non-performance on the other side, he was thinking of mutual covenants, and of the fear of non-performance arising *afterwards* owing to some new action taken by the other party. But when I promise, from fear of losing my life, that I will obey a conqueror, there is no question of his promising anything in return; and if I continue to fear that he may at some time take my life, the position is no different from what it was in the first place when I made the promise. Hobbes is therefore justified in distinguishing this situation from the one in which he allowed that a later cause of fear can make a covenant invalid. I think he also has an important point for political theory. Although we should commonly say, as the tradition of jurisprudence says, that a man is not bound to keep a promise made under duress, yet Hobbes's view is exemplified by the usages of war. At the end of a war the representatives of a conquered nation are often required to sign an instrument of surrender laying down conditions to which they agree. Many of the conditions are unwelcome, but less so than continuance of the war. The conquered nation agrees to the conditions from fear of suffering worse things at the hands of the conqueror if the war goes on. The agreement is therefore made under duress. Nevertheless the conditions of the agreement are held to be binding even after the conqueror has withdrawn his troops. Perhaps it is wrong to say that the conquered nation makes a *promise*, but at any rate the signing of an instrument of surrender is using a device very like a promise, and it is a device that has been adopted for the same reasons as the device of promising, namely, mutual convenience. It is immaterial whether or not we use the name of a promise or covenant to describe the submission of a conquered group; and therefore it is immaterial that Hobbes departs from ordinary moral and legal thinking when he says that a covenant made from fear is valid. What does matter is that he has pointed out to us the undoubted fact of politics that submission to a conqueror, though made under duress, gives rise to an obligation that continues when the immediate cause of fear has been removed.

In Chapter 15 Hobbes describes additional laws of nature. He begins with the third law of nature, that men ought to perform their covenants. On my interpretation of Hobbes, this 'ought' is a hypothetical obligation, as in all the other laws of nature, and is different from the non-hypothetical obligation of covenant itself.

Hobbes goes on to say again that the notions of justice and injustice are tied up with the notions of performing or not performing covenants. But in a state of nature, because there is no security that the other party to a contract will perform his side of the bargain, it is always possible that one is no longer validly obliged, in which event it will not be correct to call non-performance unjust. Consequently there cannot be a real place for justice and injustice until a commonwealth is set up to enforce covenants. 'So that the nature of justice, consisteth in keeping of valid covenants: but the validity of covenants begins not but with the constitution of a civil power, sufficient to compel men to keep them: and then it is also that propriety [i.e. property] begins.'

Hobbes next considers arguments for and against the view that keeping covenants is in accordance with reason, i.e. is in one's interest. His main argument is that a man may find it to his interest in the short run to break a particular covenant, but not in the long run. For no man is strong enough to rely on himself for ever; and if a man does not co-operate with others, he will suffer for it in the end.

There is no need to comment in detail on any of the other laws of nature listed in this chapter. They are in fact the usual rules of social morality: gratitude, mutual accommodation, forgiveness of injuries, treating everyone equally, and so on. (In talking of equality, Hobbes cannot let slip the opportunity of taking a side-swipe at Aristotle. Aristotle preaches inequality, says Hobbes, in holding that only wise men are fit to command while others are fit to serve, meaning that philosophers like himself are superior persons in their own conceit.) The important point is that, although Hobbes's laws of nature, other than the first two, express common rules of social morality, they are all based by Hobbes on self-interest.

Having listed them, Hobbes sums them up under the rule: 'Do not that to another, which thou wouldest not have done to thyself.' Some scholars have said that this version of the Golden Rule, as given by Hobbes, being in a negative form, is inferior to the positive form of the Golden Rule of the New Testament. In fact Hobbes's use of the negative form in this place has no significance. In Chapter 14 Hobbes explicitly identified the foundation of the second law of nature with the 'law of the Gospel', which he then stated in positive terms ('Whatsoever you require that others should do to you, that do ye to them'), and also with the 'law of all men', which he gave in a negative form

(*Quod tibi fieri non vis, alteri ne feceris*). Again, near the beginning of Chapter 17, Hobbes sums up the laws of nature in the positive rule of 'doing to others, as we would be done to'. Obviously Hobbes does not think there is any substantial difference between the positive and negative forms of the so-called Golden Rule. The important thing is not whether the rule be expressed positively or negatively, but what it is based on. Hobbes bases it on self-interest. That is where his version is substantially different from the doctrine of the Bible.

Towards the end of Chapter 15, Hobbes says that, in a state of nature, where there is no security that men will act as reason dictates, the laws of nature do not necessarily oblige *in foro externo*, i.e. in overt action; but they always oblige *in foro interno*, i.e. they always require us to desire that they be followed. Hobbes next says that the elucidation of the laws of nature is true moral philosophy. And he ends with the point that strictly speaking these rules can be called 'laws' only if we think of them as commands of God; but even then they are still obeyed, in Hobbes's view, for reasons of self-interest.

Chapter 16 gives Hobbes's account of authority. If I authorize another to act on my behalf, I make myself the author of his acts, and he acts by authority. This account prepares the way for Hobbes's description of the social contract, in which the citizens authorize the sovereign to act on their behalf. The point of the doctrine is that, if the subjects are the authors of what the sovereign does in their name, they cannot, without self-contradiction, repudiate what he has done. For it is to be deemed what they themselves have willed.

Hobbes also makes some remarks in this chapter about representation and about the justification of decision by majority opinion. He first points out that one man may represent many authors. Here of course he has in mind monarchy. He then goes on to say that if the representatives consist of many men (as in democracy, where the government is an assembly), the decision or will of the authors must be taken to be conveyed by the opinion of the majority of the representative assembly. If there is a vote of, let us say, sixty against forty, Hobbes argues that the forty votes on the second side are cancelled out by forty votes on the first side, and the twenty votes left on the first side remain uncancelled, so that these must be taken to constitute the voice of the group as a whole.

In Chapter 17 Hobbes repeats his view that the prudential obligation of the laws of nature, and the contractual obligation of covenants, are ineffective in a state of nature because men's natural passions are too strong to be restrained by mere reason or the weak bonds of words. In such a situation what we find is the code of honour only; and this is illustrated in international relations. Therefore a *common power* is needed to force men to obey the laws of nature.

Hobbes then proceeds to describe the social contract. A common power can be set up if men make a contract with each other in the following terms: everyone promises to give up his right of self-government to a particular man or assembly of men, authorizing him or it to act on behalf of the person promising; and, in accordance with the second law of nature, the promise is conditional upon others doing the same. In this way the multitude can be united in one artificial person, the State, Leviathan, the 'mortal god'. The person who is given authority is called the *sovereign*, and those who authorize him become his *subjects*. There are two ways in which sovereign power may be attained, (1) by agreement, and (2) by force. A State set up in the first way may be called a 'commonwealth by institution'. A State set up in the second way may be called a 'commonwealth by acquisition'.

Chapter 18 describes the rights of the sovereign. The most important point is that these rights are not limited by any contractual obligation. The social contract is made by the citizens with one another. The sovereign makes no covenant, and therefore he has no artificial obligations. There is no question of his acting in breach of covenant, i.e. unjustly. Since every citizen is the author of the sovereign's acts, in the sense that Hobbes has explained in Chapter 16, a citizen who complained of injury by the sovereign would be complaining of injury by himself, since he himself is author of the act complained of; and it makes no sense to talk of doing injury to oneself (i.e. of acting unjustly towards oneself, since the term 'injury' here means unjust action and not simply harm). Hobbes notes that the sovereign may be said to commit iniquity, but not injustice or injury. The reason why the sovereign may be said to commit iniquity is that equity (treating people equally) is prescribed by one of the laws of nature, and the sovereign is (naturally or prudentially) obliged by the laws of nature. If he does not follow the laws of nature, the State will collapse, which will be bad for him as for the rest. But all the duties of the sovereign are hypothetical or natural obligations.

At the end of the chapter Hobbes argues that sovereignty must be undivided. Otherwise, he says, there will be the danger of civil war, as there was when Parliament claimed part of the sovereign authority and wanted to limit the prerogative of the king. Then again, Hobbes argues, religious dissenters who claim liberty of religious worship independently of what the sovereign allows, are liable to cause civil war, as happened in the Scottish revolt against the Book of Common Prayer. Hobbes considers the objection that the condition of subjects is miserable if the sovereign is given absolute, undivided authority. His reply is that, however tyrannical a government may be, this is a lesser evil than the state of nature, civil war. In short he urges peace at any price.

Chapter 20 discusses commonwealth by acquisition. Hobbes begins by pointing out the similarities between an acquired and an instituted commonwealth.

First, in both cases the motive for accepting dominion is fear. In an instituted commonwealth men enter it from fear of each other; in an acquired commonwealth men accept it from fear of the sovereign. With both types a covenant of obedience may be assumed, and the fact that the covenant was made owing to fear does not render the covenant invalid.

Secondly, the rights of the sovereign are the same in both cases. The sovereign has absolute authority, and cannot be accused of injustice, for he has made no covenant.

Moreover, the subject is in the same position in both cases. For, although in an acquired commonwealth there has been no social contract, nevertheless the subject must be assumed to have promised the sovereign that he will obey so long as his life is spared. Otherwise he could not be called a subject but only a captive. We may compare the distinction between a servant and a slave. Captives and slaves are not under obligation to their master. A subject is, just as a servant is.

> It is not therefore the victory, that giveth the right of dominion over the vanquished, but his own covenant. Nor is he obliged because he is conquered . . . but because he cometh in, and submitteth to the victor; nor is the victor obliged by an enemy's rendering himself, (without promise of life,) to spare him for this his yielding to discretion; which obliges not the victor longer, than in his own discretion he shall think fit.

In Chapter 21 Hobbes discusses two kinds of liberty. First, there is a brief account of what Hobbes calls 'natural liberty'. This gives Hobbes's view of free will and determinism. Secondly, Hobbes deals with 'the liberty of subjects', i.e. political liberty.

Natural liberty concerns what *can* be done through one's own agency. If I am made to do something by some external agency, I do not act freely but act under compulsion. Irrespective of whether I act freely or under compulsion, in either case I act *of necessity*, i.e. my action has a cause. But if *I* am the cause, then it is proper to say that *I* do the action, or that I *can*, that I have the power to, do it.

By contrast, the liberty of the subject concerns that which a person *may* do, that which he is permitted to do by the laws or by virtue of his natural right. An action which I am free to do in this sense is opposed to an action which I am obliged not to do. If I am obliged by the law not to steal, I am not free to steal, in the sense that I do not have a right, a licence, to steal. But it is still possible (though not permissible) for me to steal. I *can* break the law; I have the power to do so, and if I do, my action is free in the sense that I caused it, I was not compelled by an outside cause.

Hobbes's general definition of liberty or freedom is the absence of opposition or external impediments. He points out that natural liberty according to his definition is not confined to human beings. We may speak of non-human animals, and even of inanimate objects, acting freely. Water in a lake that is not confined by a dam is free to run off in a stream. A stone may be said to fall freely if there is nothing to restrict its motion. Similarly a free man is a man who is not prevented by chains or prison bars or any other impediment from doing what he wills or wants to do. It does not make sense to say that the will is free. If a man's will or wish is not opposed by anything outside, so that he can do what he wants to do, the *man* may be said to be free. Yet what is done freely is done necessarily. It is part of a causal chain and so happens necessarily.

The second kind of freedom is freedom from 'artificial bonds', the bonds of artificial obligation. Because these are only metaphorical bonds, with no real strength in them, a man *can* break them, even though he is not *permitted* to do so. That is to say, he has freedom in the first sense, natural liberty, but not in the second sense, legal or moral liberty. (We might even call it 'artificial liberty' by contrast with 'natural liberty', though Hobbes himself uses only the second of these expressions and not the first.) Legal and moral liberty, the liberties of the subject, can be divided into two classes. First, there is the class of actions which the civil laws do not forbid. I may do whatever I have not been forbidden to do. Secondly, there is the class of actions which I have a right to do because I cannot be obliged in regard to them. Even if the sovereign enacts a law saying that I should kill or wound myself, or that I should deliberately run the risk of being killed, I am not obliged to obey this law, for my covenant did not extend to any such obligation. My right or licence in this case derives from that part of my original natural right which I have not given up. It is indeed psychologically impossible for me to will my own death, and so impossible for me to covenant to this effect.

Chapter VI

Criticism

(1) METHOD

In Hobbes's method, as applied to moral and political philosophy, there appears to be a confusion between causes and reasons, between explaining and justifying. His avowed procedure is that of science, which aims at explaining phenomena by tracing their causes. This procedure can certainly be applied to the study of man and society, and when it is so applied, one is pursuing social science. Psychology, anthropology, sociology, economics, political science, are all attempts to study human behaviour scientifically, tracing causal connections. When Hobbes looks for causal connections between human nature (the psychology of motives) and civil war, he is doing social science; and there is no reason why he should not. But social science is not the same as social (including political) philosophy.

Philosophy is not concerned with tracing causes. It is concerned (i) with the analysis of concepts, and (ii) with the critical evaluation of beliefs in which those concepts are used. Hobbes is doing political philosophy when he gives us definitions of key concepts, when he suggests that there are different senses of a concept, e.g. liberty, and when he traces the logical relations between different senses or different concepts. He is also doing political philosophy when he attempts to justify absolute sovereignty and political obligation, i.e. when he gives us *reasons* why we *ought* to obey the State. Now there is absolutely no reason why a man should not engage in both social science and social philosophy. Indeed there is every reason why he should combine social science with the first, analytic, function of social philosophy. A social science that does not go along with the logical analysis of key concepts is liable to be confused; and a social philosophy that takes no account of human behaviour and of existing institutions is liable to be a castle in the air. There need be no conflict or confusion between the tracing of causal connections and the analysis of concepts. The trouble arises when the second function of philosophy, the normative function of giving justifying reasons for the acceptance or rejection of beliefs, becomes mixed up with the scientific task of tracing causes. There need not be a conflict between philosophical justification and scientific explanation, but the relation between them is rather obscure and it is easy to confuse the two.

This is what Hobbes appears to do in his account of obligation. When he speaks of natural obligation playing upon the motive of fear, he thinks of obligation as a form of causal power. Similarly, when he speaks of artificial obligation as constituting only a weak bond, he again is thinking of the 'bond' as a causal factor that is too weak to be relied upon. At the same time, however, his theory of political obligation is an attempt to give us reasons why we *should* obey the State, rather than causes explaining why we *do*. The fact is that we don't, always; hence the need to give us reasons why we should.

To give a man reasons why he should do something is to presuppose that he has a choice, that he can rationally decide between alternatives. That is, it presupposes free will. Hobbes in fact holds that there is no free will, that everything we do is necessitated. This is because he thinks that everything can be causally explained, explained as following necessarily from causal laws. If he had seen clearly that to give justifying reasons is a different thing from setting out explanatory causes, he would have found his determinism less tractable.

The reason why he fails to distinguish adequately between explaining and justifying lies in his attachment to geometry. He thinks that causes are the same as logical grounds, in the way that the definitions of Euclid are grounds for the conclusions of theorems. Now the relation between causes and logical grounds is a complex problem for the theory of knowledge. We need not go into that here. In order to understand Hobbes's position, it is sufficient to note that the logical grounds of a theoretical conclusion constitute reasons for accepting that conclusion. So it was natural for Hobbes to suppose that reasons for a *practical* conclusion, which are indeed also grounds for that conclusion, are the same sort of thing as reasons or grounds for a theoretical conclusion. And since he identified geometrical reasoning with tracing the effects of causes, it was equally natural that he should confuse causal explanation with the giving of reasons for doing something.

It is easy enough to say that causal explanation is not the same as rational justification. But it is not at all easy to say just what the relation between them is. In criticizing Hobbes for confusing the two, I am not complaining that he misleads us. On the contrary, I think we are indebted to him for enabling us to see that there is a difference. It is only when a result of mixing up causes and reasons comes out sharply, as it does in Hobbes's philosophy, that other philosophers can start trying to disentangle them. We should also remember that Hobbes is, as I said in expounding his method, the first thinker to put forward explicitly the idea of social science in its modern sense. Social science cannot take the place of social philosophy in the job of critical evaluation, but it can take and has taken the place of speculative ideas about the nature of man and society which once formed part of philosophy. It is understandable that the greater success of scientific methods than of the older philosophical methods in this latter field should lead men to think that scientific method can be applied successfully to the whole of the traditional province of philosophy. It is understandable, though it is not now excusable. It was excusable in Hobbes, since he was the first to make the attempt. Part of the point of studying the work of a philosopher like Hobbes is to enable us to see what scientific methods can do, and what they cannot do, and so to enable us to draw more clearly the distinction between the explanatory function of science and the analytic and critical functions of philosophy.

(2) METAPHYSICS

Hobbes's metaphysical theory of strict materialism quickly breaks down. We need not spend much time in criticism of it, since the weakness of Hobbes's metaphysics does not really affect the force of his moral and political theories. They depend more on his psychology and a weakness *there* is more crucial. If his psychology were sound, it could stand without the materialist metaphysics, apart from the one point that there would be less reason to adopt determinism, since determinism is the application to psychology of mechanism, i.e. of the sort of process that we suppose to be involved in the behaviour of material things.

Hobbes's materialism breaks down both for the concept of life and for that of mind. Hobbes assumes that a living thing differs from inanimate matter only in its power of self-movement, for which he gives a materialist explanation. But other essential features of living organisms are the powers of reproduction and self-repair. These are not explained in Hobbes's account.

As regards mind, Hobbes holds that all elements of consciousness are mere appearances of physiological matter in movement. But to say that physiological movement appears as an image prompts the question: to whom or to what does the image appear? To say that X appears as Y, is an incomplete sentence. It is implied that X appears as Y to Z. This is not just a trivial verbal point that happens to apply to the word 'appears'. It applies to most of the words which Hobbes uses to express his view of consciousness. He says that elements of consciousness are 'appearances', 'seemings', 'fancies', 'images'. To say that X seems to be Y implies that it seems so to someone. To say that it is a fancy implies that someone is fancying. In the case of the word 'image', the objection is greater still. Hobbes holds that we do not really perceive external objects; we really undergo physiological motion, and perceive this as an image of the external object that is affecting us. Here again, as before, we may ask who or what does the perceiving. But we may also ask: how can we or Hobbes say that what we perceive is an image of an external object if we are unable to perceive *both* and compare them? If we never perceive external objects, how can we know that there are any external objects or know that our sense-contents are images, i.e. resemblances of them?

There are, then, two objections to Hobbes's account of perception. First, his theory implies that there is a mind or self over and above the sense-contents, a mind or self to which physiological movement 'appears' as something external. This mind or self cannot also be appearance of physiological motion; for if it were, there would have to be a further self to which the first one 'appears', and so on *ad infinitum*. Secondly, Hobbes's account is inconsistent in implying both that we are never aware of external objects and that we are aware of external objects. He implies that we are never aware of external objects when he says that all our mental contents are images or appearances. Yet in holding that they are images of external objects, he implies that they can be seen to resemble external objects, which presupposes that we can be aware of external objects so as to compare them with the images.

However, even if strict materialism is dropped, it is still possible to say that the mind, though different from the body, is entirely dependent on the workings of the body. This is not strict materialism, which holds that only matter exists, but the revised theory (epiphenomenalism) still makes matter and material process fundamental. If Hobbes had been an epiphenomenalist, he would still have thought that determinism followed from his metaphysics, in that everything which happened in the mind would be causally dependent on what happens necessarily in the body. But apart from the determinism, Hobbes's moral and political theory need not depend even on the modified metaphysics of epiphenomenalism.

(3) PSYCHOLOGY OF ACTION

Hobbes's psychology of action is open to two main criticisms. They concern (a) egoism and (b) determinism.

(a) *Egoism*
The egoistic psychology which is to be found in Hobbes's early work, and especially in *Human Nature*, is modified in his later writing, so

that the explicit statement of his psychology in *Leviathan* cannot be called egoistic. Nevertheless the effects of the earlier doctrine can still be seen in some details of Hobbes's moral and political theory, with the result that it is still beset by grave weaknesses.

It is Hobbes's view that the fundamental endeavour of every man, and indeed of any organism, is self-preservation. From this it follows that a deliberate decision to take one's own life, or to sacrifice one's life for the sake of others or for an ideal cause, is literally impossible. If a man does take his own life, or does sacrifice or risk his life for the sake of others or for an ideal, Hobbes will have to say that it was not deliberately intended. Either the man miscalculated the probable consequences for himself, or else he was not in his right mind so that he was not able to think rationally at all.

This is notoriously not what we commonly think. We should all admit that selfishness is, generally speaking, a predominant human motive, but there certainly are many cases where a person is prepared to sacrifice his own interest, or even his life, for the sake of other persons or for an ideal. Even animals will sometimes sacrifice themselves for the sake of their young. Of course our commonsense interpretation of motives in such cases may be illusory, but in order to accept the view that it is, we need to be given strong evidence. Hobbes does not offer any strong evidence. He is working with a hypothesis of fundamental motivation and he is interpreting the facts to fit his hypothesis. This is why he says, of apparently altruistic motives like benevolence and pity, that they depend on egoistic motives. You can go a long way in this direction, but not all the way. For example, when Hobbes says that pity, defined as grief at the calamity of another, depends on the interested motive of fear that a similar calamity may befall oneself, it is relevant to point out that one may feel pity when it is impossible that the same calamity may befall oneself. Adam Smith gives a good example when he says that a man may sympathize with the pain of a woman in child-birth. Or I may feel sorry for a child who is suffering from measles when there is no chance of my getting measles in the future. Or again one may feel sorry for a parent's loss of a young child when one's own children have already had a good span of life or if one has no children and is unlikely to have any in the future. It may be said of some examples that it is not strictly impossible for the same calamity to befall oneself; for instance, it is not impossible for me to have measles again. But the point is that I do not think I shall get measles again, and so I cannot be afraid of getting measles when I pity the child who is ill.

Hobbes's egoism is the result of two things. First, it results from the observation that egoistic motives certainly do play a predominant part in human life. But this does not prove that all motives are egoistic. I think that Hobbes came to see this himself by the time he wrote *Leviathan*. Secondly, Hobbes's egoism results from his attempt to assimilate the laws of human behaviour to the laws of mechanics: specifically, to assimilate human motivation to the law of inertia, to the effect that a body always tends to continue in its present state of motion or rest, so that a living thing always endeavours to go on living. But this is contrary to experience both of men and of other animals; and we have seen that on other grounds it is a mistake to reduce the behaviour of living things to that of inanimate things.

(b) *Determinism*

Hobbes rightly distinguishes between freedom from external constraint and freedom of the will. He allows the former and denies the latter. To say that a man is free to do what he chooses is not to say that he is free to choose. Hobbes denies freedom of choice. He holds that everything which happens happens necessarily, is caused. An action may be caused by desire (and then it is free in the sense of free from external compulsion), but it is still necessarily caused. Consequently Hobbes holds that the will is simply a form of desire.

The chief objection that can be made to determinism is that the idea of obligation implies a choice. To say that a man is obliged to do X, or ought to do X, implies that he has the choice of either doing it or not doing it. This is incompatible with saying that he must necessarily do X. If Hobbes is going to talk about obligation at all, as he certainly wants to do, he should in consistency abandon determinism. The reason why he fails to see this is that he confuses obligation with determination. He contrasts obligation and freedom, and says (in Chapter 14) that obligation or law 'determineth, and bindeth' to one course of action. Now it is obvious that, even on Hobbes's own account of obligations, an obligation does not in fact necessarily determine an action. This is certainly true of artificial obligation, which is not a real bond but mere 'words and breath', easily broken. Hobbes has allowed for that: this sort of so-called obligation is a kind of fiction, not a real obligation in the sense of a determining force. But it is also true of natural obligation that it does not necessarily determine. The laws of nature state obligations which *would* be necessarily followed by men *if* they were purely rational. Since men are in fact more motivated by their passions than by reason, they cannot be relied upon to follow the obligations of natural law unless these are backed by fear of physical force.

Hobbes fails to see the difficulty here because he contrasts obligation with liberty. But we need to distinguish liberty or freedom in the sense of what one *may* do from liberty or freedom in the sense of what one *can* do. Obligation is opposed to liberty in the sense of what one *may* do, but not in the sense of what one *can* do. If I am obliged not to hit another man on the head, I am not free to do so in the sense that it is not morally or legally *permissible* for me to hit him on the head. But this does not imply that I *cannot* do it, that I do not have the power to do it. On the contrary, to say that I am obliged implies that I do have that power.

In a way Hobbes recognizes that 'ought' implies 'can'. He sees that if I am to have an obligation not to do X, then refraining from X must be something which I can do. This is why Hobbes thinks it does not make sense to speak of an obligation of non-resistance. Human nature is such that a man cannot have a motive for non-resistance; he will necessarily resist an attack on his life. So it is impossible for him to refrain from resistance. Therefore we cannot speak of his being obliged to refrain from resistance. This is not in his power, and 'ought' implies 'can'. But Hobbes does not allow for the further fact that obligation also implies the power to do the opposite. To say 'I ought to do X' implies both that it is in my power to do X and that it is in my power to refrain from doing X. It implies that I have a choice of either course. That is to say, it implies liberty or freedom – in Hobbes's words, 'liberty to do, or to forbear'. Hobbes fails to see this because he notes that obligation removes the liberty to do or to forbear and binds to only one of these. But what this means is that when I am obliged, I no longer *may* take either course of action. It does not mean that I no longer *can* take either course of action.

(4) MORAL THEORY

I select two main points for comment under this heading: first, Hobbes's account of good and evil; and secondly, his account of obligation.

(a) *Good and evil*
Good and evil are defined by Hobbes as the objects of desire and aversion respectively. In his view, good and evil are always relative and never absolute. In our ordinary use of the terms, sometimes they are clearly relative, as when we speak of someone's good, meaning his interest, which may or may not be quite identical with what he desires but which certainly must have some relation to his desires and his satisfactions. At other times, however, we use the terms 'good' and 'evil' in ways that at least seem to suggest a non-relative meaning. In consequence many philosophers have held that there is such a thing as absolute or intrinsic goodness.

In considering whether Hobbes's account is satisfactory for usages that suggest an idea of intrinsic goodness, we need to make a distinction between moral goodness and non-moral intrinsic goodness. We may speak of virtue as being good, meaning that it is morally good; and we may speak of a man as good, again meaning morally good. This sense of 'good' is connected with the idea of moral obligation. To say that virtue is morally good is to imply that it is the sort of thing that ought to be pursued. And to call a man morally good is to imply that he usually does the sort of thing that ought to be done. Now when Hobbes defines the worth or value of a man purely in economic terms, this is inconsistent with the moral use of the word 'good' when we speak of a good man. On the other hand, Hobbes is in that place talking of 'natural' conceptions of evaluation, before any thought of artificial obligation comes into the picture. And since artificial obligation is his version of categorical obligation, it follows that his account of the value or worth of a man is not the concept that we have in mind when we speak of a morally good man, since the latter concept is tied up with the idea of categorical obligation.

We also appear to use the term 'good' in a non-relative way which is different from the idea of moral good that I have just been discussing. For instance, we may say that knowledge, or the pursuit of knowledge, is good for its own sake; or that the creation and appreciation of beauty is good for its own sake. When we make statements such as these, we do not, I think, imply that there is any moral obligation to pursue knowledge or to produce or appreciate beauty.

Now it is possible to say of this sense of good that it is related to human desires. It is possible to say that the pursuit of knowledge is good (i) because knowledge is useful in promoting human happiness, and (ii) because all or nearly all human beings have the desire of curiosity. Hobbes himself, it will be recalled, speaks of curiosity as a feature distinguishing human beings from other animals, and he seems to regard this as a disinterested desire, that is, as not being tied to the pursuit of self-preservation. Similarly, one may say that the value of beauty lies in the fact that all human beings enjoy aesthetic creation and appreciation in some form. What is not possible is to say that the desires which make us value knowledge and beauty are self-interested. Knowledge is valued because it benefits mankind in general and because we realize that nearly everyone has the motive of curiosity. Likewise with beauty. As I say, Hobbes himself, in speaking of curiosity, thinks of it as a disinterested desire, i.e. as a desire which is not dependent on the procuring of happiness for oneself alone. His definition of good and evil, however, does seem to make them self-interested notions, and insofar as it does this it is defective. Here again we see that Hobbes's mistake is due to the egoistic character of his account of *practical* notions. Even though the egoistic psychology is modified in *Leviathan*, the heritage of Hobbes's original egoistic psychology continues to invalidate important parts of his moral theory.

(b) *Obligation*

It is often said that Hobbes has only an egoistic conception of the notion of obligation as well as of good and evil. According to my interpretation, this is not the case. Hobbes's theory does contain a distinction between two kinds of obligation, one prudential or egoistic or hypothetical, the other not. The fact that he has this distinction is a considerable merit. Furthermore, if the distinction can be made without recourse to 'nonnatural' or 'transcendental' properties, this will be welcome, since the scheme will be simpler and more intelligible than one in which there is talk of non-natural or transcendental properties. For Hobbes, nonhypothetical obligation is non-natural in the sense that it is artificial, a matter of *words*, in which we *talk as if* there were a bond, but without the necessity of saying that there really is a mysterious impalpable bond.

Hobbes's account has the further advantage of pointing out to us the similarity between such obligation and logical necessity. We saw that Hobbes thinks of natural obligation as being a form of causal necessitation, and this is a mistake, a mistake made by anyone who supposes that acting from a motive, such as desire, is being *caused* or necessitated by that motive. Now just as Hobbes regards natural obligation as a form of causal necessitation, so he regards artificial obligation as a form of logical necessitation. His distinction between natural and artificial obligation carries with it a distinction between two types of necessity. He regards natural obligation as a form of causal necessity; but he treats artificial obligation as a form of merely logical necessity, a matter of logical consistency. To break an artificial obligation is a matter of contradicting yourself. This is an interesting and valuable suggestion because logical necessity, like obligation, is not a real necessity at all. It is perfectly possible to be inconsistent. If a man accepts the premisses of a valid argument, we say that he 'must', or 'ought to', accept the conclusion. For instance, if he accepts the premisses that all philosophers are crackpots and that Hobbes is a philosopher, we say he 'must' accept, or 'is bound to' accept, the conclusion that Hobbes is a crackpot. But of course it is perfectly possible for him to say that he does not accept this. We may call his decision irrational, but it can be taken. In this way, logical necessity is like obligation. They are both thought of as 'musts', and yet they are not real necessities. There is therefore at least an analogy between obligation and logical necessity.

Nevertheless I think that Hobbes's account is inadequate for two reasons. The first reason is that obligation is not *just* the same as logical necessity. The second reason is that Hobbes confines this type of obligation, non-hypothetical obligation, too narrowly to the case of promises.

(i) To see that moral obligation is not just the same as logical necessity, let us look at the type to which Hobbes confines himself, the obligation to keep promises. This is certainly the most helpful type of case from his point of view. It is, I think, correct to say that a man who breaks a promise is, in a sense, involved in a practical self-contradiction. As we say, he 'breaks his word'. He expresses an intention to act one way, and then acts a different way. But this is not all that is involved. For what has been described so far is true not only of breaking a promise but also of breaking a resolution. Suppose I make a New Year resolution to take a cold bath every morning. On 1 January, I leap out of bed and into my cold bath. Comes 2 January – I crawl out of bed, turn on the cold tap, shudder, and turn the tap off again. I have broken my resolution. I have contradicted in action the intention that I have expressed. But would we say that I have broken a moral obligation? Would I feel that I have failed in my moral duty? I might well feel *ashamed* of my irresolution, but I should not feel *remorse*, such as I should feel if I had broken a promise. What is the difference? It is that a promise involves another person. My New Year resolution simply concerns myself. A promise concerns another person, and this makes a considerable difference. The obligation or 'bond' to keep a promise is a bond with another person, an inter-personal tie, and this makes it a distinctive sort of thing. Hobbes's account of the obligation to keep promises omits this vital factor.

The reason why Hobbes omits this factor is because of his egoistic account of motives. A sense of obligation must be able to serve as the motive of action, and a promise differs from a resolution in that it concerns the doing of something for another person, so that the sense of obligation to keep the promise is the thought of having engaged myself to do something for another. Hobbes in his original psychology would deny that this thought can serve as a motive for action, because he holds that the motive of every voluntary action is a good to oneself; and he repeats this even in *Leviathan*.

(ii) The second objection to Hobbes's account raises the same point again. Hobbes limits non-hypothetical obligation to promises, and when he considers all the other rules of social morality (such as equity, complaisance, gratitude) he bases them on self-interest. So his account of moral rules as laws of nature makes them all natural, i.e. prudential, obligations. But once we deny that self-interest is the sole motive of action, there is nothing to prevent us from taking the commonsense view that these duties – gratitude, forgiveness of injuries, equal treatment, and so on – are not dependent on self-interest, but involve the thought of an inter-personal tie with others, just as the duty of promise-keeping does. Having agreed that motives for action can be altruistic, as in benevolence, and that the sense of moral obligation can be a motive without considerations of self-interest, there is no longer any reason why one should define the words 'good' and 'evil' as Hobbes does. A good man is a man who is commended for acting from the sense of duty or from other virtuous motives such as benevolence. Again, one may approve or disapprove of things, calling them good or bad, because of their effects on others and not only because of their advantageous or disadvantageous effects on oneself.

(5) POLITICAL THEORY

The chief merit of Hobbes's political theory is that it clarifies the distinction between power and authority, and shows that the working of political institutions cannot be understood in terms of power alone. If a State is to work, there must be at least a measure of willing obedience on the part of most of the citizens. Hobbes expresses the point by the doctrine of social contract or covenant, but we need not take this too literally. Contract or covenant, if taken literally, covers naturalized citizens, founding fathers, and the signatories to an instrument of surrender, but not their descendants. The essential point that Hobbes is getting at can be better put with the notion of consent that was used by later thinkers, beginning with John Locke. Locke's idea is that if I live in a country and neither leave nor actively protest against its laws, I can be understood to consent to them; and so I am obliged to abide by them, the obligation being again a form of contractual or promissory obligation. The obvious objection to Hobbes's political theory concerns its absolutism. Why should the authority of the sovereign be absolute, so that he is permitted to do whatever he likes? And why should the subjects consent to that? In order to avoid the state of nature, Hobbes answers. But are they not leaping from the frying-pan into the fire? Locke (*Second Treatise, Of Civil Government,* §93) puts the point succinctly: 'This is to think that men are so foolish that they take care to avoid what mischiefs may be done them by pole-cats or foxes, but are content, nay think it safety, to be devoured by lions.' Accordingly Locke, in his version of the social contract, limits the authority of the government. He does it in this way. He first assumes that the citizens make a social contract with each other to set up a society. Then he assumes a second contract, or more properly a trust. In this second act of institution the citizens entrust the sovereign with the authority of office on condition that government be wielded for the common good of the citizens. So the sovereign has obligations on Locke's view; the sovereign is to be understood as having promised to protect the rights of the citizens and promote the common good. If he fails to satisfy these conditions, he has not carried out his trust and is no longer entitled to obedience; he no longer has authority, since the authority vested in him was entrusted on conditions.

Hobbes argued against a limited authority on the ground that it would lead to civil war. If king and Parliament disagreed, he thought, they would be bound to fight. This assumes that it is impossible to reach agreement without fighting: and it also assumes that nothing can be worse than civil war. Here again Hobbes's original psychology is at the root of his argument. He supposes that if there is disagreement, it is impossible, without the use of force by an *ultimate* authority, to prevent this disagreement from leading to conflict. He assumes that rational considerations alone are not enough to prevent conflict. But in fact this is not always so, as we can see in the occasional instances today where there is danger of overlap between the provinces of different authorities in the State, e.g. between the authority of the legislative power and that of the judicial power. When this happens, both Parliament and the Courts take care to keep off the treacherous ground. It was not always so. The building up of a tradition, after experience of conflict, was necessary. But still it is possible to learn from experience and to act, purely on rational considerations, in a way that prevents open conflict. Hobbes is also mistaken in his assumption that men will think nothing is worse than civil war. He takes this view because he supposes that the fear of death is the strongest motive. But men have been known to prefer death to some other things.

Chapter VII

Interpretations – I

Every great philosopher is subject to a variety of interpretations. What he does is to present familiar facts in a novel perspective. He arranges them in an unfamiliar way. The result is to throw us off our balance. We cannot simply suspend disbelief, as with a work of fiction, for the new perspective is grounded on familiar facts, on what we take to be true. Whether we try to accommodate ourselves to the new framework, or try to resist it by showing that it does not fit the facts, we are liable to distort it a little, pulling it here or squeezing it there because our old picture of the facts seems to require that. The philosopher himself may not be free from ambiguity because he too has the difficulty of adjusting all his ideas to the new outlook; he is liable to slip back at times, at least in his language, to the old ways of ordering the data.

In the case of moral and political philosophy the feeling of being thrown off balance is all the more disturbing because the ideas concern action and not just belief. Opposition to Hobbes in his own time was especially sharp because his moral and political philosophy seemed to undermine the ideas on which men relied in their practical life. It is not surprising that the interpretation of his thought in those contemporary critics should be judged mistaken by Hobbes himself and by later scholars. Differences of interpretation have persisted, however, down to this day. In fact the last few decades have seen quite a stream of books on Hobbes (mostly about his political philosophy) continuing to differ quite radically in their accounts. The extent to which Hobbes still stimulates new interpretations is a mark of his stature as a philosopher of politics.

My purpose in these last two chapters is to survey the differing interpretations given in recent works of scholarship. A main line of division is in the attribution to Hobbes of innovation on the one hand and tradition on the other. Of course, both elements are there in his work; otherwise it would not be possible for the two sets of scholars to make their respective cases. Any philosopher of importance is necessarily an innovator, precisely because significant philosophy is a matter of presenting a new perspective. On the other hand, almost any philosopher,

like almost any scientist or artist, must take something from his prede-
cessors, from a tradition of work in that field. Everyone would agree
that Hobbes said some things that were new and derived others from
tradition. The differences in the interpretations are differences of emphasis. Emphasis counts none the less. The thought of a philosopher
may be properly classed as overall traditionalist or innovatory.

The traditional interpretation of Hobbes classes him as an innovator,
and this view seems to be supported by Hobbes himself, who said (in the
Epistle Dedicatory of *De Corpore*) that the study of 'civil philosophy'
was no older than his book *De Cive*. But that statement does not necessarily contradict the interpreters who see Hobbes as a traditionalist.
When Hobbes claimed that he had placed the study of politics on a new
footing, he was probably thinking of his method; he meant that he was
the first to treat political theory scientifically, after the manner of
natural philosophy. No interpreter would deny that particular claim,
though some would question its importance. Differences of opinion
among interpreters are focused on four other issues. The first is the
relation between Hobbes's political and his ethical theory; the second is
the relation of both of these to his psychology; the third is the relation of
his ethics and politics to his general philosophy; and the fourth is the
relation of his ethics and politics to theology.

(1) POLITICS AND ETHICS

Among earlier thinkers on politics one can distinguish between the
'moralists' and the 'realists'. Those whom I am calling moralists were
concerned with the normative question of justifying the actions of
political rulers in terms of ethical values; positive law and governmental
action were justified if they pursued ethical goals such as equity and the
common good. Those whom I am calling realists were more concerned
with a non-normative inquiry, describing and explaining how in fact
political rulers behave; the account given was largely in terms of power
and self-interest. For this second approach, morality was irrelevant to
politics but if questions of justification were to be invoked they had to be
made subservient to the harsh facts: in politics might was right.
Religious thinkers, needless to say, took the moralistic view. So did pre-
Christian philosophers of a quasi-religious turn of mind, such as Plato
or the Stoics.

From a very superficial reading of Hobbes one might think that he
takes the realist view: power and self-interest are what count; in politics
might is right. Indeed Hobbes seems to go further than political realism
as I have sketched it. While realism holds that positive law or political
rule is independent of morality, Hobbes appears to say that there is a

relation of dependence but in the opposite direction to that claimed by the moralists; the rules of morality depend on the command of the political sovereign. This reading of Hobbes, however, is certainly mistaken. He does of course agree that power is essential for political rule, but he is more concerned to show that a human ruler cannot acquire enough power without the bonds of moral obligation. The relation between ethics and politics is complex. They are, in different ways, dependent on each other. Moral obligation is ineffective without the backing of 'the sword' of government, yet political power consists in great measure of the support of subjects given from a sense of moral obligation.

The moralists' view of the relation between ethics and politics can be put by saying that positive law (the law laid down by a human sovereign) depends for its validity on natural law (the principles of morality or, if morality is related to religion, the law laid down by the divine sovereign). Realists commonly reject the notion of natural law. According to them, law must be positive law, man-made, artificial. Hobbes appears to depart from realism in this respect, for he has a lot to say about natural law and it clearly plays an important part in his theory. On the other hand his idea of natural law seems to be very different from the traditional one held by Stoic and Christian philosophers. For them, natural law sets out moral obligations that every man has to his fellows. For Hobbes, the laws of nature are primarily prudential prescriptions of reason, telling a man what he must do for the sake of self-preservation. Hobbes goes on to say that, strictly speaking, they can be called laws only if they are regarded as commands of God, which comes back to part of the traditional Christian conception; but whether or not we call them laws (think of them as divine commands), the really important thing is that they function as prudential prescriptions.

In this matter Hobbes seems clearly to diverge from tradition, to use the idea of natural law in a new way; and since he says (*Leviathan*, Chapter 15) that the science of the laws of nature is the true moral philosophy, his notion of morality must be different from that of Christianity and common opinion, in which virtue is distinguished from self-interest and is largely concerned with service to others. If this is correct, then Hobbes's view is after all similar to that of realism, according to which morality is a masked form of self-interest. What is striking about Hobbes's version of the view is that he is able to spell out his prudential 'laws of nature' so that they coincide in content with the virtues of traditional non-egoistic morality.

That is the most common interpretation of Hobbes's ethics and especially of his view of natural law. But it has been challenged by some

recent scholars, most notably by Howard Warrender, who would persuade us that Hobbes belongs to the main stream of natural law theory and that his conception of natural law is the most important element of his political philosophy. In reaching this view Professor Warrender was influenced by an article of A. E. Taylor, arguing that Hobbes's view of ethics is not egoistic but 'a very strict deontology' (i.e. a theory that gives a value to duty for its own sake).

Taylor was led to his thesis by two considerations. First, he noted that Hobbes distinguishes counsel (which looks to the interest of the person counselled) from command, and describes the laws of nature as 'precepts' or commands. From this Taylor concluded that prudential thinking can only result in counsel and that precepts or commands must be non-prudential. Taylor's conclusion is in fact fallacious since Hobbes also says, in his distinction between counsel and command, that command is directed to the benefit of the commander. When Hobbes sets out this distinction, e.g. in *Leviathan*, Chapter 25, he is treating both counsel and command as addressed to another person. It is not clear that he would apply either term to the precepts a man may give to himself.

Secondly, Taylor pointed out that Hobbes writes of the obligation of covenants in terms reminiscent of deontological theory. Hobbes says that a just man is one who does what is just 'because the law commands it' and not because he fears punishment for disobedience. Hobbes also compares injustice or promise-breaking to self-contradiction, and Taylor thought this was similar to a feature of Kant's ethics, except that Kant says self-contradiction would result from a *universalization* of wrongful action. Taylor supposed that Hobbes's view of the obligations of covenant (or justice) represents his view of morality as a whole, and pressed his comparison with the later deontological theory of Kant, according to which a dutiful action must be done for the sake of duty and not from a regard to beneficial consequences, whether for the agent or for others. Here Taylor began with a crucial observation but extended it beyond the evidence in supposing that Hobbes's remarks about the performance of covenant (or justice) can be applied to morality as a whole, including the obligations imposed by the laws of nature. Hobbes's idea of practical self-contradiction is more simple and straightforward than that of Kant's ethical theory. It applies only to promise-breaking and has nothing to do with the rest of morality.

Warrender was rightly critical of Taylor's extravagant leap from Hobbes's remarks on covenant to a full-blown theory of duty for duty's sake. Warrender was more impressed by the part that laws of nature play in Hobbes's political theory and by Hobbes's statement that to be laws, properly speaking, they must be the word of God, who has a right to command. He therefore treated Hobbes as essentially a natural law theorist of the traditional type. Of course Warrender could not overlook the fact that laws of nature for Hobbes are prudential, whether or not they are also commands of God, and so he allowed that Hobbes's conception of morality has a prudential character. Even when a man treats the laws of nature as divine commands, Warrender said, Hobbes may well think of his motive as self-interested, the desire for eternal salvation; but then this is in line with some aspects of Christian doctrine and so, according to Warrender, not necessarily a departure from traditional and popular views of morality.

Another scholar who made Hobbes a traditionalist in ethics was F. C. Hood, but his evidence was far more thorough than that of Taylor and his attention to the texts more comprehensive than that of Warrender. Hood agreed that Hobbes began with a self-interested view of morality but pointed out that in his latest statements about ethics, in *De Homine*, Hobbes writes of moral virtue in terms that would be acceptable to any Christian moralist; he confines moral virtues to justice and charity, and distinguishes these from prudence, along with fortitude and temperance, on the ground that the second group seek the benefit only of the individual and not of the commonwealth. Hood also observed that the obligation of covenants in Hobbes's political theory has a special character because it is an artificial imitation of the obligation of laws of nature. Just as the State itself is an artificial imitation of nature, so is its system of law, justice, and obligation. In short, positive law is modelled on natural law, and politics is dependent on ethics as model to archetype. This is a perceptive reading of Hobbes, unfortunately neglected by most scholars because they have been put off by Hood's more general contention that Hobbes is altogether a Christian thinker.*

(2) PSYCHOLOGY AND ETHICO-POLITICAL THEORY

Earlier commentators on Hobbes almost all took it for granted that he held an egoistic theory of psychology and that this determined the character both of his ethical views and of his political ideas. In the

---

* My own distinction between natural and artificial obligations and rights is obviously close to Hood's view, though there are differences: for example, Hood treated artificial rights, like natural right, as (what I call) rights of action while I make them rights of recipience. I did not in fact derive my interpretation from Hood's book; cf. my article, 'Obligations and Rights in Hobbes', published in *Philosophy*, 1962, while Hood's book, *The Divine Politics of Thomas Hobbes*, was published in 1964. There was no converse influence either; Hood was unaware of my article when he wrote his book.

recent literature this has been questioned and we can now say confidently that the earlier view was too simple. The history of the change in interpretation is curious and interesting.

A distinction must be drawn between psychological egoism and rational egoism. Psychological egoism is a theory about human psychology; it states that every man necessarily and always acts from the motive of maximizing his own interest. Rational egoism is not a theory of what does and must happen; it is a doctrine of what it would be rational to do – of what, in a sense, one ought to do; it states that the rational course of action on all occasions is to maximize one's own interest. Because rational egoism can be framed in terms of 'ought', some theorists call it ethical egoism. The 'ought' is a prudential, not a moral 'ought', but a person who advocates rational egoism usually holds that it states *all* that one ought to do, so that for him there is no different kind of 'ought'. Strictly speaking, rational egoism is incompatible with psychological egoism. For to say that a man ought to do one thing, even if the 'ought' expresses simply a rational imperative and is not what we should normally call a moral imperative, is to imply that he has a choice between doing that one thing and some other thing. 'You ought to maximize your own interest' implies both that you can do so and that you can fail to do so. Psychological egoism on the other hand leaves no room for choice; it says that a man must necessarily act from the desire to maximize his own interest. But of course a theorist can fail to notice the incompatibility, and several philosophers, Hobbes among them, have been accused of doing so.

For a long time commentators thought it was obvious that Hobbes was a psychological egoist. It also seems fairly plain that his account of the laws of nature makes him a rational egoist. The laws of nature represent prescriptions of reason telling us what we must do to preserve our lives, what we ought to do as a matter of prudence. Hobbes tells us that the science of them is the true moral philosophy, so it seems that for him rational egoism is also ethical egoism. Although it is not consistent to hold this position together with psychological egoism, people often try to defend rational egoism as the standard of ethics by arguing that there is no alternative because all action must be motivated by self-interest. This is why it was supposed that Hobbes's psychology determined the character of his ethics. In the same sort of way it was thought to determine his political doctrine also. Psychological egoism results in competition and the state of war. When a commonwealth is set up, the sovereign needs to have absolute power because his egoistic subjects must be kept in line all the time by fear of unpleasant consequences.

Hobbes's account of the natural condition of mankind as a state of war was widely criticized by his contemporaries. But the specific attribution to him of a theory of psychological egoism dates from comments of Bishop Butler in the eighteenth century (described in Chapter 5 above). Butler's criticism of Hobbes, in two long footnotes appended to Sermons 1 and 5 of *Fifteen Sermons preached in the Rolls Chapel*, impressed scholars as masterpieces of concise refutation. It was taken for granted that they correctly represented, and thoroughly disposed of, Hobbes's view of human nature. How then could one account for the uncannily persuasive force still exerted by Hobbes's theory as a whole?

The correct answer to that question is that Butler's criticism applies only to *Human Nature*. The two footnotes are intended to refute Hobbes's account of charity and of pity. Butler quotes from *Human Nature*. It is natural that he should do so, for the first three of his sermons are on the subject of human nature. He says nothing to show whether he had read *Leviathan*. Certainly he was unaware that Hobbes's definitions of charity and pity in *Leviathan* are significantly different from the descriptions of them in *Human Nature*. Scholars who did read both works simply failed to see the difference; they assumed that Hobbes's view remained unchanged and that Butler's refutation stood sound.

As we have already seen, A. E. Taylor perceived that some of Hobbes's statements about ethics were puzzling if one accepted the conventional view that he was a psychological and a rational, or ethical, egoist. Taylor's solution to this problem was to deny that Hobbes was an ethical egoist, while still accepting that he was a psychological egoist. Taylor claimed that Hobbes's ethical theory was deontological, which meant that the motive for morally commendable action could not be self-interest. But Taylor, who greatly admired Bishop Butler, did not question the conventional account of Hobbes's psychology. So he put forward the hypothesis that Hobbes's ethical theory was logically unconnected with his psychological theory; Hobbes was trying to answer two separate questions, why men ought to obey the law and what inducements were needed if a sense of obligation was ineffective. Taylor did not explain how the sense of obligation as a motive could be fitted into a theory of psychological egoism.

Howard Warrender made a more ingenious suggestion. In his interpretation of Hobbes there is not, as there is in Taylor, an incomprehensible gap between ethics and psychology, for Warrender did not treat Hobbes's ethics as a deontology. Nevertheless he did think that 'Hobbes's theory of political society is based upon a theory of duty, and his theory of duty belongs essentially to the natural-law tradition' (*Political Philosophy of Hobbes*, p. 322), and so he could not regard

Hobbes's ethics as a straightforward theory of rational egoism. Accordingly he distinguished 'two systems' in Hobbes's theory, a 'system of motives' and a 'system of obligations'. The system of motives explains how a man *can* do his duty (because he sees it as a means to his preservation), and the system of obligations explains why he *ought* to do it (because it is the will of God). The will of God is the 'ground' of obligation, the desire for self-preservation is a 'validating condition' of it. Warrender's distinction between grounds and validating conditions of obligation was worked out with great care, but it is open to criticism. Warrender agreed that in the end the reason why a man ought to obey the will of God (which is tantamount to saying that the ground of his obligation) is prudential.

More recently David P. Gauthier has produced another sort of distinction to relate Hobbes's psychology to his ethics. Like Warrender, Gauthier argued that in one sense the ethical theory does, and in another sense it does not, depend on the psychology. Where Warrender wrote of two systems, Gauthier produced two sets of definitions of ethical concepts: the 'formal' definitions (analysing one ethical concept in terms of another, e.g. 'a right' as 'an absence of obligation') are un-affected by the view anyone might take of the actual character of human motivation, while the 'material' definitions depend on Hobbes's egoistic psychology. In principle this programme is similar to that of Warrender and is open to similar criticism. Against Warrender it has been argued (e.g. by J. W. N. Watkins) that a complete statement of the ground of obligation would include validating conditions; against Gauthier it can be argued that complete definitions of Hobbes's ethical concepts must include material as well as formal elements. Gauthier would no doubt agree with this. His point is to deny Taylor's thesis that the moral theory is independent of the psychological, while at the same time making allowance for the evidence that Taylor brought forward.

But the whole enterprise is misguided. Before the publication of Gauthier's book, F. S. McNeilly demonstrated that Hobbes set out an explicitly egoistic psychology only in *Human Nature* and moved away from it as he developed his political theory in *De Cive* and *Leviathan*. Bernard Gert followed this up and pointed out that the process of development is carried still further in *De Homine*, where Hobbes's ethical views (as F. C. Hood had noted) are close to traditional Christian doctrine. There is therefore no need for the accounts of Taylor, Warrender, and Gauthier in order to explain the relation between a strictly egoistic theory of psychology and Hobbes's more impressive accounts of ethics and politics.

(3) GENERAL PHILOSOPHY AND ETHICO-POLITICAL THEORY

Hobbes expounded his metaphysical theory of materialism fully in *De Corpore*, published in 1655. But he had reached it before he wrote his political works, and its implications for psychology are lightly sketched at the beginning both of *Elements of Law* and of *Leviathan*. Hobbes presumably had no doubt that everything built on his psychology could be reduced to materialistic terms. In fact, however, he hardly ever refers to the supposed materialistic base once he gets going with the development of psychological and ethical concepts and with constructing his political doctrine in the light of these. Consequently a number of interpreters believe that the ethical and political theories do not really depend on the materialist metaphysics and should be considered independently. A straightforward version of this account was given by G. C. Robertson in an admirable little book, published in 1886, that dealt with all aspects of Hobbes's thought. The same view was taken in a slight early work by A. E. Taylor and a far more substantial one by John Laird, both of whom, like Robertson, considered the whole of Hobbes's philosophical writings with no special emphasis on the political theory.

A more arresting account was given by Leo Strauss in an important book (*The Political Philosophy of Hobbes*, 1936) that did concentrate attention on Hobbes's political theory. Strauss agreed with Robertson that the 'main lines' of Hobbes's political doctrine were fixed before he thought out his mechanistic philosophy, but Strauss went a good deal further than that. Hobbes's general philosophy is reflected in the political theory not only as a theory of knowledge and reality but also as a doctrine of method; Hobbes believed that the method of science was the right method of acquiring knowledge in any field. Now Strauss argued that what Hobbes derived from natural science contributed nothing of real importance to his political philosophy. The method no less than the metaphysics was irrelevant.

Strauss's book is less persuasive now than those of some more recent commentators, but it was a landmark in the history of the interpretation of Hobbes's ethical and political theory, and especially in the history of discussion whether Hobbes was an innovator or a traditionalist. Strauss noted that while most readers take the former view, one or two commentators had pointed to traditionalist elements in Hobbes's thought. John Laird in particular, Strauss wrote, had maintained 'that in ethical and political theory Hobbes's "voice and hands are both mediaeval" ' (*Political Philosophy of Hobbes*, p. xi). Laird was in fact contrasting Hobbes's metaphysics with his ethics and politics. He said that in metaphysics Hobbes's 'voice' (i.e. his doctrine) was modern, while his 'hands' (i.e. technique) 'were scholastic and even Aristotelian', but in ethics and politics both were medieval, being derived from civil and canon law. Nevertheless, Laird allowed, Hobbes 'may have done more than any other Englishman of his time to break the older order of political theory and, as he claimed, to innovate profoundly' (*Thomas Hobbes*, p. 57).

Strauss set himself to trace the development of Hobbes's ethical and political theory. He concluded that Hobbes acquired his basic political doctrines from a reading of history, and especially from his study of Thucydides in early life. He then turned to science and as a result acquired a materialistic metaphysics and the belief that the method of science should be applied to the study of man and society. The *exposition* of his political theory therefore took a scientific form, in which everything was supposed to be connected together logically, the account of man being built up from the account of matter, and that of society from that of man. The importance and originality of Hobbes's political philosophy, however, according to Strauss, owe nothing to that idea. Strauss said in his Preface that 'the particular object' of his book was to show that 'the real basis' of Hobbes's political philosophy does not lie in the inspiration of science, neither in the metaphysical materialism nor in the scientific method. What then was important and novel in Hobbes's political theory ? According to Strauss, 'the ideal of civilization in its modern form, the ideal both of the bourgeois-capitalist development and of the socialist movement, was founded and expounded by Hobbes with a depth, clarity, and sincerity never rivalled before or since' (*Political Philosophy of Hobbes*, p. 1). Hobbes began with an Aristotelian and aristocratic ethic in which honour has the highest place; he then came to be critical of this and replaced it with a 'bourgeois' ethic of justice.

Strauss's thesis has been criticized as historically inaccurate, e.g. by Raymond Polin, who maintained that 'Hobbes is neither an aristocrat, nor a bourgeois, but a conservative' (*Politique et philosophie chez Thomas Hobbes*, p. 150). Polin argued that Hobbes never gave his own support to an aristocratic ethic and that it is anachronistic to talk of a 'bourgeois' concept of virtue in the seventeenth century. Strauss would probably agree with the latter remark; his point was rather that, from the historical perspective of the twentieth century, we can look back and view Hobbes's values as the harbinger of the bourgeois attitude.

The suggestion, which seemed so questionable to Polin, was taken up with enthusiasm by C. B. Macpherson, who brought the tools of Marxist analysis to the interpretation of the political theory of Hobbes (and of Locke). Far from thinking it an anachronism to use the term 'bourgeois', Macpherson argued that the society in which Hobbes lived was indeed already a bourgeois society and that Hobbes's supposed picture of natural man was derived from that society; Hobbes's individualism, no less than his values, reflected the ethos of bourgeois society.

Unlike Strauss, Macpherson claimed that Hobbes's novel outlook on ethics and politics is closely linked with his general philosophy, that in fact bourgeois individualism is necessarily connected with mechanical materialism. Hobbes's 'leap in political theory' was 'as radical as' Galileo's new approach to mechanics; it derived the ideas of rights and equality from 'the need of each human mechanism to maintain its motion' (*Political Theory of Possessive Individualism*, p. 77). The interpretation itself needed a (politically) radical leap of scholarship, and it is doubtful whether Hobbes would have recognized Macpherson's picture of Hobbesian men as self-moving 'mechanisms' or 'machines'. Although Hobbes was a materialist and therefore believed that men and animals, like everything else, consist of matter in motion, he kept clear the distinction between the natural and the artificial. In the Introduction to *Leviathan* he said that we may call a machine an artificial animal and the State an artificial man; he did not say that animals and men are natural machines.

A less radical case for linking Hobbes's political theory with his general philosophy was made by J. W. N. Watkins. He allowed that Hobbes's views on psychology and ethics cannot be deduced from materialism, but claimed that the character of the political theory is determined by the general nature of Hobbes's philosophy and especially by his conception of scientific method. The method is the resolutive-compositive method of Galileo, exhibiting the structure of a thing by first resolving it into its parts and then composing it again from those parts. Hobbes uses the method in his political theory, according to Watkins, by resolving the State into its component parts of independent individuals without the bonds of law and justice, and then reconstituting the State from those parts by the device of a social contract. Watkins regarded his thesis as a criticism of the position of Robertson and Strauss, but I am not sure that they would have regarded it so. Robertson said, and Strauss agreed, that Hobbes's political 'doctrine' had its main lines fixed before Hobbes became a mechanical philosopher. This is not to deny that after he became such a philosopher Hobbes expounded the political doctrine by a scientific method. Strauss did indeed deny that the method contributed anything to the real importance of Hobbes's political philosophy, but then he and Watkins took different views of what constitutes the importance of Hobbes's political theory. Later commentators have in any event tended to agree that, while Hobbes writes of the resolutive-compositive method in *De Corpore*, the method he espoused in *Leviathan* is modelled instead on the method of geometry.

A further claim made by Watkins concerned Hobbes's nominalism. Nominalism is the philosophical theory that there are no universal entities, no such things as common qualities, but only 'names' or words that are applied to a number of individuals; for example, a tomato and a pillar-box do not share a common quality of redness but we can apply the same word 'red' to both of them. Watkins claimed that Hobbes's nominalism was responsible for a nominalist account of authorization, indeed a 'nominalist theory of the state', because Hobbes's sovereign is authorized to act 'in the name of' his subjects. F. S. McNeilly has shown, however, that Hobbes's nominalism is not a strict nominalism, and that in any case nominalism does not and cannot play the part assigned to it by Watkins in Hobbes's account of authorization.

The more general point made by Watkins concerning the influence of scientific method was followed up by M. M. Goldsmith, who presented Hobbes's political theory as part of a general scientific enterprise in which the method of science is applied to all fields of inquiry, including civil philosophy. Goldsmith concluded that the point of Hobbes's political theory was scientific explanation of the phenomena of law, religion, and history. This seems to imply that it did not have a practical purpose, and if so, Goldsmith has been misled by Hobbes's assimilation of philosophy to science.

The views of Strauss, Polin, Macpherson, Watkins, and Goldsmith present an unbroken line of debate, which I have not wanted to interrupt for reasons of chronology. Between the publication of Strauss's book (1936) and Polin's (1953), however, there appeared an essay by Michael Oakeshott that must be mentioned separately. It was a long introduction to Professor Oakeshott's edition of *Leviathan*, published in 1946. Like all Oakeshott's writings, it impresses the reader both by its imaginative style and by glimpses of a novel vista. But the vista is seen through a glass, darkly, and it is not easy to say just what Oakeshott's interpretation comes to. On the relation of Hobbes's political theory to his general philosophy, Oakeshott disagreed with all the then current views. It was a mistake, he wrote, to think that the political philosophy followed from or was determined by the materialist metaphysics. It was equally mistaken to think that Hobbes intended such a relation but failed to sustain it. It was even a mistake to treat the political philosophy as a science of politics; for Hobbes, in Oakeshott's view, was well on the way to the modern distinction between science and philosophy, the first seeking a knowledge of the phenomenal world, the second seeking a theory of knowledge itself. Hobbes's civil philosophy is connected with his general philosophy, Oakeshott maintained, because they are both philosophy, and philosophy for Hobbes is essentially reasoning. Oakeshott went on to describe this reasoning as being concerned with causes and effects, but he nevertheless distinguished it from science, apparently because science proceeds by observation, with the implication (unless I have misunderstood) that science therefore cannot, or that Hobbes thought it cannot, proceed by reasoning also. So Hobbes, in Oakeshott's view, is a 'rationalist'. It is right to think of his political philosophy as part of a system, but wrong to think of the system as analogous to an architectural structure. The systematic character of Hobbes's thought lies in 'a guiding clue, like the thread of Ariadne', the application throughout of a particular conception of philosophy.

A recent book by Thomas A. Spragens has applied to Hobbes a view about tradition and innovation that was originally expounded by Thomas Kuhn in his account of the history of science. According to Kuhn, a revolution in scientific theory consists of the transformation of a 'paradigm', a model that has captured allegiance over a long period. Spragens, finding a number of Aristotelian elements in Hobbes's philosophy, claimed that Aristotle's thought was a paradigm for Hobbes as it was for most medieval philosophers, but that Hobbes subjected it to a transformation. The trouble with this interpretation is that the concept of a paradigm is rather vague. As I wrote at the beginning of this chapter, every philosopher of note introduces a novel perspective and almost every philosopher builds on the thought of the past. One can say that not only Hobbes but also his contemporaries Descartes and Spinoza transformed an Aristotelian paradigm, but this image adds little except to suggest that the history of philosophy follows the same sort of pattern as was traced by Kuhn for the history of science. Spragens claimed that Aristotle was a paradigm for Hobbes because of similarities in the metaphysical views of the two philosophers. The comparison was overdrawn, however, because Spragens knew more of Hobbes than of Aristotle and tended to bring Aristotle's thought nearer to that of Hobbes than an Aristotelian scholar would do. Spragens conducted his case mainly in terms of metaphysics but argued that the concept of motion in Hobbes's metaphysics determined the character of his political theory.

(4) THEOLOGY AND ETHICO-POLITICAL THEORY

Many of Hobbes's contemporaries called him an atheist. They may not have meant that he was deliberately lying when he talked as if God existed; but what he said about God was so bizarre, as compared with Christian orthodoxy, that they could not think it a credible form of religion. Modern commentators have mostly been divided between two views, one that Hobbes wrote about theology with his tongue in his cheek, the other that he was sincere enough but nevertheless enjoyed outraging the orthodox. An interesting feature of recent interpretation is the claim by two or three scholars that Hobbes's political theory is founded on traditional Christian doctrine. The claim goes along with the view that his ethical doctrine is equally Christian and traditional, a view that I have already discussed in talking of the relation between ethical and political theory.

A. E. Taylor's article was largely confined to Hobbes's ethical doctrine. Taylor connected ethics with natural law and of course treated natural law as the word of God. He therefore concluded that Hobbes's philosophy involved some kind of genuine theism, but did not insist on its being traditionally Christian.

Howard Warrender's interpretation attributed to Hobbes a traditional form of Christian theology as well as of ethics. Warrender did not press this very far and was ready to agree that in many respects Hobbes's account of theology was distinctly unusual. But he emphasized the dependence of moral obligation on the will of God in Hobbes's theory, with the consequence that atheists cannot be morally obliged. When Warrender asked himself what was the ground of the obligation to obey the will of God itself, he put forward two possibilities: one was that this obligation was in a sense prudential, being grounded on the desire for salvation; the other was simply that God's right to be obeyed was 'axiomatic or ultimately mysterious' (*Political Philosophy of Hobbes*, p. 301). Warrender regarded his first alternative as more probable, but he was seriously ready to contemplate that Hobbes, of all people, might have accepted religious mystery as the ultimate foundation of his system.

F. C. Hood went further still. The general theme of his book is that Hobbes's political doctrine depends on Christian belief, that his view of morality is Christian despite first appearances, that the lengthy arguments from the evidence of Scripture are perfectly sincere, and that Hobbes's originality lies in his method, not in his doctrine, though he is of course peculiar in trying to combine Christianity with materialism. This is a surprising interpretation, and most scholars interested in Hobbes seem to have rejected it as clearly mistaken. But it is worth noting that Hood's account arose not from, but in the face of, initial prejudice. In the Preface to his book, Hood wrote that for more than thirty years he shared the common view of Hobbes as 'a mechanist, to whom a prime mover could be little more than a logical requisite', whose use of Scripture was ironical, and who 'identified duty with interest'. A scholar who felt obliged to go back on all that as the result of close and extensive study of Hobbes's texts should not be simply dismissed.

Nevertheless, the most impressive of more recent interpreters, McNeilly and Gauthier, have both taken the view that Hobbes's theology can be discounted. McNeilly produced a delicious phrase for it: Hobbes 'preserved theology only by pickling it in political vinegar' (*Anatomy of Leviathan*, p. 24). Neither of these two scholars has argued his case on this point in any detail – presumably they thought it unnecessary – but they have backed it up with a little evidence. For example, McNeilly pointed out that when Hobbes says the laws of nature are properly called laws only if regarded as commands of God, this comes, in a single sentence, right at the end of a long discussion of the character and content of the laws of nature; its function, therefore, is *dismissive* of the theological view of them. Gauthier, in a brief footnote, thought that Hood's interpretation could be refuted simply by referring to another remark of Hobbes about the laws of nature made in answer to criticisms of Bishop Bramhall. McNeilly's view, it would seem, is that Hobbes's theology was not meant to be taken seriously. Gauthier's opinion is less extreme; he wrote that God plays a part, though only a secondary part, in Hobbes's system and that Hobbes was a believer, not an atheist.

Chapter VIII

Interpretations – II

The survey given in Chapter 7 has concentrated on certain aspects of dispute about tradition and novelty in the philosophy of Hobbes. Inevitably it has neglected other points of importance in recent interpretations. I shall now therefore list in chronological order the more significant of these interpretations, with bibliographical details, and in certain instances I shall add a note of some features that have not been mentioned already.

With one exception, my list is confined to works written in English, but I have the impression that no serious loss is occasioned thereby. Among older works there is a valuable book in German by Ferdinand Tönnies about Hobbes's life and thought in general, but it has little bearing on the controversies of more recent years concerning the interpretation of Hobbes's political philosophy in particular.

My list is also mainly limited to books. Needless to say, there are many important articles to which the student can be referred with profit, but they mostly deal with matters of detail while I am concerned here with interpretations in the round. Three of the books listed below were each preceded by an article in which the author set out a central element of his interpretation. In these cases it is appropriate to include the article as well as the book. The list also includes A. E. Taylor's article because of its influence on the very important book by Warrender and because some later commentators couple the two together in talking of the 'Taylor-Warrender thesis'.

George Croom Robertson, *Hobbes* (Edinburgh and London, 1886)
Despite its age, Robertson's book is still well worth reading. It is especially interesting on Hobbes's life, and is comprehensive, though succinct, on his thought. It does not contain a great deal on the political theory.

Frithiof Brandt, *Thomas Hobbes' Mechanical Conception of Nature* (Copenhagen and London, 1928)
As the title suggests, this book is entirely about Hobbes's metaphysics

and his contributions to physics. It says nothing about his ethics and politics. For the student of Hobbes's metaphysics it is a work of the first importance. In its close attention to the actual texts it may well have afforded a model for one or two of the more recent works of scholarship about Hobbes's political theory.

John Laird, *Hobbes* (London, 1934)
Like Robertson, Laird deals with all sides of Hobbes's thought. The book is a scholarly one and is especially helpful as a contribution to the history of philosophy, noting possible influences on Hobbes and (in more detail) the influence of Hobbes on later thinkers. It is not particularly useful on the political theory, however; Laird appreciates that Hobbes's political theory is outstanding but does not make clear *why* it is.

Leo Strauss, *The Political Philosophy of Hobbes* (Oxford, 1936)
Strauss's book sparked off the remarkable series of novel interpretations of Hobbes's political philosophy that have appeared in recent decades. He begins by noting that a couple of scholars (Laird, Dilthey) have called Hobbes a traditionalist, although most think that he is an innovator and that the revolutionary character of his political theory depends on the attempt to produce a *science* of politics. Strauss's procedure is to give a historical account of the development of Hobbes's thought. He produces evidence for the following conclusions. (a) Hobbes began as a traditionalist, accepting much in Aristotle (especially from the *Rhetoric*) and also accepting an aristocratic code of virtue. (b) Hobbes then turned from philosophy to history (his translation of Thucydides) for normative guidance on politics. Thereby he was led to found his moral and political ideas on the twin psychological bases of pride and fear, and this psychological framework is what really determines his new view, which represents a transition from aristocratic to bourgeois virtue. (c) Finally Hobbes turned back from history to philosophy again, but a new kind of philosophy. Through coming to know something of geometry and the natural science of Galileo, he decided that a true philosophy should be scientific, i.e. exact, and so he now rejected Aristotle, who had maintained that practical sciences cannot be exact. According to Strauss, Hobbes reverts from Aristotle to Plato (who believed in the possibility of an exact science of morals and politics) but with criticism of the content of Plato's views.

This account takes in the traditional aspects of Hobbes's thought, while at the same time accepting the more common view that Hobbes was an innovator. It allows for Hobbes's own belief in the importance of a science of politics, yet maintains that the really revolutionary character of his political philosophy does not depend on a scientific approach but on the psychological framework that Hobbes derived from his study of history. In noting that Hobbes's support for absolute government goes along with an adhesion to 'bourgeois' (instead of aristocratic) morality, Strauss indicates, more persuasively than Macpherson was to do later, how far a Marxist approach to Hobbes is justified.

A. E. Taylor, 'The Ethical Doctrine of Hobbes', *Philosophy*, 1938; reprinted in *Hobbes Studies*, edited by Keith C. Brown (Oxford, 1965)
The gist of Taylor's article has been given in Chapter 7. Its merit lies in having drawn attention to the peculiar character of the obligation of covenants in Hobbes, and the historical importance of the article lies in its influence on Warrender.

Taylor wrote a slight general work about Hobbes many years earlier (*Thomas Hobbes*, London, 1908), but this is of no particular consequence for understanding the ethical and political theory.

Michael Oakeshott, Introduction to his edition of *Leviathan* (Oxford, 1946); the Introduction is reprinted, with other essays by Oakeshott on Hobbes, in *Hobbes on Civil Philosophy* (Oxford, 1975)
Oakeshott's view of the relation between Hobbes's political theory and his general philosophy has been sketched earlier. In discussing the political theory itself, Oakeshott thinks that Hobbes is a leading representative of a tradition of political thought based on the ideas of Will and Artifice, to be contrasted with the 'Rational-Natural tradition' that produced the concept of natural law. On the particular issue of political obligation, Oakeshott argues that Hobbes has three senses of obligation, physical, rational, and moral, and that political obligation is a combination of all three.

Raymond Polin, *Politique et philosophie chez Thomas Hobbes* (Paris, 1953)
I have already mentioned in Chapter 7 that Polin criticizes as anachronistic Strauss's attribution to Hobbes of a bourgeois concept of virtue. He also questions Strauss's contention that Hobbes originally espoused an aristocratic morality. He argues pretty convincingly that Strauss's evidence for this view is inadequate. Hobbes certainly describes an aristocratic morality in which honour has a high place, but this does not imply support. Polin holds that the evidence does not allow us to trace any definite historical progression in Hobbes's views.

On the relation of ethics to politics Polin writes this: 'The politics of Hobbes does not have a moral foundation. Or rather, the moral foundation of his politics is that a moral foundation for a political philosophy does not exist' (p. 151). That is to say, Polin reverts to a view held by Hobbes's early critics.

Richard Peters, *Hobbes* (Harmondsworth, 1956)
This Pelican paperback is a stimulating and helpful survey of all the different aspects of Hobbes's thought. Peters's own interests are most marked in his treatment of Hobbes's psychology. On motivation he follows Strauss in stressing pride and fear. The account of Hobbes's political philosophy is not especially notable, except that the theory of sovereignty is related to Hobbes's view of law in an interesting way, and both the political and the legal theory are enlightened by presentation of the historical background. Peters believes that the distinctive conception of Hobbes's theory of social contract is to join individualism with absolutism, an individualist foundation with an absolutist conclusion.

Howard Warrender, *The Political Philosophy of Hobbes: His Theory of Obligation* (Oxford, 1957)
Warrender's book is most impressive and made a considerable impact on scholars, even though it won few adherents. I have given some account of its main theme in Chapter 7 and shall now add a little more; but it is really impossible to do justice to this book in a brief summary, because it compels admiration for the care with which Warrender has worked out a logical framework of interlocking concepts, something that can be appreciated only by reading the book as a whole.

Warrender argues that essentially the political philosophy of Hobbes belongs to traditional natural law theory. Men are obliged by the laws of nature, which are the commands of God. This is moral obligation. Its ground is the will of God, and if we ask why ought we to obey the will of God, the answer is either 'for the sake of salvation' or a mystery. The first alternative (which Warrender seems to prefer) makes morality in the end a matter of self-interest. Warrender agrees that Hobbes describes the laws of nature as being more immediately in our interest, but he denies that this consideration gives them any obligatory force. He distinguishes the ground of obligation (the reason why an action is obligatory) from the validating conditions of obligation (the circumstances in which the obligation applies), and he maintains that the immediately prudential character of natural law is a validating condition and not the ground of obligation; when I see that seeking peace is a necessary means to self-preservation, this gives me a motive for acting, it affords a reason why I *can* seek peace, but it does not give me a ground of obligation, it does not afford a reason why I *ought* to seek peace.

Since moral obligation depends on natural law and on the fact that natural law is the command of God, Warrender rejects the view that moral obligation arises only in the State. The difference made by the existence of the State is to provide security for those who act morally; in the condition of nature there is no security. Consequently, in the condition of nature many moral obligations are not binding in fact; their application is 'suspended' because the validating conditions of obligation are not fulfilled. The laws of nature prescribe, for example, the keeping of covenants provided that you do not thereby become a prey to others. In the state of nature the proviso does not often hold, and so the obligation to keep covenants becomes effective only when backed by the force of the civil law.

Despite the careful thinking that has gone into Warrender's system of concepts, he is curiously blind to a number of facts and possibilities that make his interpretation questionable. For example, he supposes that people who treat Hobbes's laws of nature as dependent on human psychology must be thinking of them as descriptive (scientific laws stating what must happen) and not prescriptive (injunctions of what should be done or avoided); if the laws of nature are prescriptive, Warrender assumes, they must be moral (as contrasted with prudential) laws. Again, his account of rights (and consequently of duties) is vitiated by identifying freedom from obligation with freedom from the possibility of obligation. He treats the duties of the sovereign as moral obligations corresponding to rights of the citizens arising from covenant (instead of as prudential obligations imposed by natural law), and so infers that the sovereign is a party to the covenant, at least in the case of acquired commonwealth. He is led by his theory to postulate an improbable conjunction of two, logically independent, systems in Hobbes's theory, a system of motives and a system of obligations, which coincide in effect but only contingently. (This is no doubt due to the influence of Taylor's article.)

The best feature of Warrender's book is his analysis of what Hobbes means by obligation *in foro interno*, which applies in the state of nature. Warrender's pinpointing of this feature of the theory does succeed in showing that morality is not the creation of the political sovereign, that Hobbes does not believe might is right, that Hobbes grounds morality on something other than political power even though political power is necessary in order to sustain it.

Warrender's book is also the first to examine the texts of Hobbes's political theory with the meticulous care that they deserve. He has been followed in this by other scholars. Earlier interpreters of the political theory, even Strauss, had painted their pictures with a broad brush.

C. B. Macpherson, *The Political Theory of Possessive Individualism: Hobbes to Locke* (Oxford, 1962); this book was preceded by an article, 'Hobbes Today', first published in the *Canadian Journal of Economics and Political Science*, 1945, and reprinted, under the title 'Hobbes's Bourgeois Man', in *Hobbes Studies*, edited by Keith C. Brown

Macpherson builds on Strauss's attribution to Hobbes of 'bourgeois morality', and brings a Marxist perspective both to his interpretation and to his criticism of Hobbes's views. He argues that Hobbesian man in a state of nature displays not just innate but also socially acquired characteristics; Hobbes gives us a picture of social man with the restraint of law removed. Further, the socially acquired characteristics – the dispositions to compete and to amass power and possessions – are acquired in only one particular type of society, which Macpherson calls 'possessive market society', i.e. a society which makes a market not only of the products of labour but of labour itself. Hobbes's morality is the morality of the market. Macpherson also thinks, as I have explained earlier, that Hobbes's moral and political theory depends on his materialist metaphysics.

In criticism of Hobbes, Macpherson finds two weaknesses. First, Hobbes mistakenly supposes that the traits of market society apply to any society and so are true of man universally. This error, however, does not greatly matter, Macpherson says, because Hobbes's conclusions do apply to man in market society. The second weakness is that Hobbes, in concentrating on the fragmenting effects of market society, failed to attend to the contrary effect of cohesion within classes that is produced by class distinction. Hobbes claimed that the sovereign must have the power of choosing his successor, since otherwise the society would fall to pieces; but Hobbes did not realize that the power and self-interest of the ruling class would provide cohesion. The second fault, Macpherson maintains, is a serious one. His critique is obviously influenced by Marxist doctrine.

Macpherson relies heavily on Hobbes's statement, in *Leviathan*, Chapter 10, that 'the *value*, or WORTH of a man, is as of all other things, his price'; but Macpherson neglects the deliberately satirical tone of this remark and the context of a non-bourgeois morality of honour. Again, Macpherson overemphasizes the desire for commodious living among the factors that make for distrust and war. Hobbes himself subordinates the desire for commodious living to the desire for self-preservation, but Macpherson does not allow for this.

The one-sidedness of Macpherson's interpretation is brought out by Keith Thomas, 'The Social Origins of Hobbes's Political Thought', in *Hobbes Studies*, edited by Keith C. Brown. Thomas cites evidence to show that Hobbes's own ethical views were by no means altogether friendly to a bourgeois morality, that he retained some sympathy for aristocratic virtues, and that Macpherson takes no account of the importance for Hobbes of curbing pride, a feature of Hobbes's theory that is certainly not a product of the market.

Despite its excessive vulnerability to criticism, Macpherson's interpretation is nevertheless a stimulating one and well worth reading.

F. C. Hood, *The Divine Politics of Thomas Hobbes* (Oxford, 1964)
The main themes of Hood's interpretation have been given in Chapter 7. I think this book should be taken more seriously than it has been. It is based on a closer knowledge of the relevant texts – of *all* the texts relevant to Hobbes's political theory – than any other scholar has shown. While treating the English version of *Leviathan* as the definitive text for Hobbes's civil philosophy, Hood continually compares it with the Latin rendering and with the earlier statements of Hobbes's theory in *Elements of Law* and in both the Latin and the English versions of *De Cive*. From this the reader gets a persuasive explanation of the differences between the different texts.

More important is the fact that much of the detail of Hood's interpretation does not depend on his general thesis about the Christian character of Hobbes's views. To my mind the most striking feature of Hood's account is his emphasis on a distinction between natural and artificial justice. Civil law, like the State itself, is artificial, an imitation of the natural. By covenant men create artificial obligations and rights, an imitation of the natural obligations and rights of natural law. The system of artificial justice (civil law) depends on the natural obligation of natural justice (morality), and the natural system depends on its lawgiver, God. I find this interpretation attractive because it is similar to my own view, reached independently, of a distinction between natural and artificial obligations and rights. Hood's use of the distinction between the natural and the artificial is of wider scope than mine, and in view of his extensive knowledge of the texts I should not feel in the least confident that, where we diverge, my view is preferable to his.

Although Hood's interpretation is vastly different from Warrender's, he may well have been influenced by Warrender in basing natural law on the will of God. At any rate he resembles Warrender in treating Hobbes as a traditionalist on natural law and on the relation of morality to religion.

J. W. N. Watkins, *Hobbes's System of Ideas* (London, 1965); this book was preceded by an article, 'Philosophy and Politics in Hobbes', first published in the *Philosophical Quarterly*, 1955, and reprinted in *Hobbes Studies*, edited by Keith C. Brown
In the Preface Watkins says that his book poses the question, 'How

much of Hobbes's *political* theory is implied by his *philosophical* ideas', and that 'The conclusion it reaches is that the essentials of his political theory are so implied'. But it seems to me that Watkins does not in fact show much of the political theory to be so implied. In his first chapter he allows that Hobbes's interpretation of the Puritan Rebellion (i.e. his understanding of contemporary *history*) was responsible for certain essentials of the political theory. Watkins's main concern is to stress the importance in Hobbes's political theory of the scientific method that is used in his general philosophy also. It is not clear, however, just what method Watkins is attributing to the political theory. On the one hand he says much of the resolutive-compositive method of Padua, used by Galileo and Harvey, which Watkins regards as a 'traditional' method, to be contrasted with the 'new' methods of Bacon and Descartes. On the other hand he agrees (p. 68) that Hobbes prefers the method of Euclidean demonstration, which is not the method of Galileo and Harvey. Watkins concludes from his discussion of method that the resolutive-compositive method of Padua led Hobbes to construct a well-ordered society from its citizens, its own constituents, and not from something external, so that the authority of the sovereign rests on the consent of the citizens and not on the will of God. But is it true that the doctrine of popular consent is implied by the method? It would be perfectly *possible* to say that composition from constituent elements requires divine intervention. Hobbes's alternative hypothesis of a social contract is more interesting, and more convincing to the mind of a secular age; but in his own day, and indeed much later, his device of a social contract made by inherently egoistic individuals seemed incoherent. Quite an effort is needed to render it coherent when one considers the details of 'transferring natural right'. If it can be made coherent, it is a *tour de force*; but that is due to Hobbes's inventiveness, not to his use of the method of Padua.

It is not clear to me that Watkins shows any other of Hobbes's characteristic political doctrines to depend on the general philosophy. In the earlier article Watkins says that Hobbes's subjectivist view of ethics follows from nominalism. In the book he adds that the account of authorization in Hobbes's political theory is nominalist, but this latter claim, as I have mentioned in Chapter 7, is shown by McNeilly to be unsound.

Watkins thinks he has refuted the views of Robertson and Strauss by establishing that the essentials of Hobbes's political theory are implied by his general philosophy. What are the essentials of Hobbes's political theory? (1) An emphasis on undivided sovereignty; (2) a realization that political authority depends both on consent and on force; (3) the device of a hypothetical state of nature and a hypothetical social contract in order to make clearer the truth of (2). Watkins admits that (1) came from

Hobbes's understanding of history. He claims, I think unsuccessfully, that (2) came from Hobbes's scientific method. It is reasonable to say that (3) came from that source. As I have indicated in Chapter 7, this last point does not touch Robertson, who said that Hobbes's political 'doctrine' was formed independently of his metaphysics; (3) is not a political doctrine but a (certainly powerful) expository device. The point does touch Strauss, who denies that scientific method contributed anything of importance and who presumably would deny (as I would not) that this expository device is one of the really important things in Hobbes's political theory.

M. M. Goldsmith, *Hobbes's Science of Politics* (New York and London, 1966)
Goldsmith's book is an especially useful one for the elementary student of Hobbes's political theory. The exposition is clear and readable, and when Goldsmith reviews controversial interpretations of particular issues he is always sensible and often shrewd in his judgements. His view of the relation of the political theory to Hobbes's general philosophy has been described earlier.

F. S. McNeilly, *The Anatomy of Leviathan* (London, 1968); this book was preceded by an article, 'Egoism in Hobbes', published in the *Philosophical Quarterly*, 1966
For the student of *philosophy*, McNeilly's book is the best of recent discussions of Hobbes. Most of the modern commentators limit themselves to exposition of what they take to be Hobbes's views, and refrain from asking whether the argument and evidence supporting those views are sound or unsound, no doubt because they think the latter enterprise misguided in dealing with a thinker of the past. (This is not true of all of them. Macpherson couples interpretation with critical appraisal; and Hood, although trained as a historian and not as a philosopher, is quite ready to say that Hobbes has made a mistake in this place or that.) McNeilly is not only prepared to criticize Hobbes; he is also the most competent of the modern commentators to do so. At the same time, criticism of Hobbes does not prevent McNeilly from recognizing the force and merit of his theory. Although the strictly political part of Hobbes's philosophy is treated only in the last chapter of McNeilly's book (some 40 pages out of 250), this chapter gives a more penetrating appreciation of the nub of Hobbes's political theory than does any other commentary. So many of the commentators say that Hobbes is a great political theorist but do not explain why. McNeilly does. But just because McNeilly is an acute philosopher, his book is hard going for someone who lacks training in philosophy. The reader who can follow

the argument, however, will find much enjoyment in the book; for it is written with style and a gaiety of example not often found in social studies and not all that often in philosophy either.

McNeilly observes that *Leviathan* differs from the other statements of Hobbes's political theory, *Elements of Law* and *De Cive*, in two important respects. (1) *Elements of Law* and *De Cive* imply an egoistic psychology, while *Leviathan* does not. (2) *Elements of Law* and *De Cive* are not conducted with any definite method of inquiry, while *Leviathan* is a firm attempt to follow the demonstrative method of mathematics. McNeilly links these two points together.

As regards (1), McNeilly distinguishes between a firm theory of psychological egoism (to be found in *De Corpore* and derived from Hobbes's mechanism) and 'pessimism', a practical expectation, derived from experience, that men will generally act from self-interest. *Elements of Law* and *De Cive* display the pessimistic view. They also emphasize 'glory', the desire to be pre-eminent over others, as if this were chiefly responsible for the state of war, although Hobbes adds, briefly, in *De Cive* that 'the most frequent' reason for violence is something different, competition. In consequence, the purported argument from egoism to the state of war is confused. *Leviathan*, by contrast, does not give expression to egoism, or to pessimism either. Hobbes may well have retained a privately pessimistic view of human nature, McNeilly adds, but he does not express it publicly. Charity and pity are given straightforward definitions in the usual altruistic terms, as contrasted with the egoistic definitions of *Elements of Law*. Again, *Leviathan* defines power and glory in a neutral manner without necessarily implying comparison with other men.

As regards (2), McNeilly argues that Hobbes's views about method in *Elements of Law* and *De Corpore* are confused but that in one part of *De Corpore* he gives what is virtually a hypothetico-deductive account of physics, according to which the conclusions of physics are merely provisional and are never demonstrated as final truths. By contrast, the propositions of mathematics are both demonstrable and true. In *Leviathan*, McNeilly continues, Hobbes is still not clear of confusion since he talks both of demonstration from definitions and of proceeding from psychological experience, but in the main he aims to follow the method of mathematics.

McNeilly then puts the two points together. Hobbes's method in *Leviathan* required him to reach his political theory by deduction from definitions about human nature. Since the egoistic psychology of *Elements of Law* and *De Cive* did not lead by clear deduction to the conclusions that the political theory requires, Hobbes abandoned (or made no use of) the egoistic psychology in *Leviathan*. Hobbes's science of politics in *Leviathan* is a formal system setting out what is implied by rational deliberation. What matters most for such deliberation is the uncertainty of success in achieving your aims without an ordered society. The question of just what your aims are is not so central as it appeared to be when Hobbes wrote the earlier versions of his political theory.

This approach makes Hobbes very much a modern thinker, and it is not surprising that McNeilly should discount the place of theology in Hobbes's system.

McNeilly's first point, the abandoning of egoism in *Leviathan*, was originally set out in his article of 1966. The same sort of view has been put forward by Bernard Gert in an article, 'Hobbes and Psychological Egoism', first published in the *Journal of the History of Ideas*, 1967, and reprinted in *Hobbes's Leviathan: Interpretation and Criticism*, edited by Bernard H. Baumrin (Belmont, California, 1969). Gert goes further than McNeilly in that he denies that Hobbes was ever a psychological egoist.

David P. Gauthier, *The Logic of Leviathan* (Oxford, 1969)
I have already discussed in Chapter 7 Gauthier's view of the relation between Hobbes's ethics and his psychology. This is not, however, the most important feature of Gauthier's book. Gauthier is most impressive in what he has to say about authorization. He points out that the authorization of the sovereign does not appear in *Elements of Law* (or the printed version of the second part of that work, *De Corpore Politico*) or in *De Cive*. It is an innovation in *Leviathan* and, according to Gauthier, it is 'Hobbes's enduring contribution to political thought' (p. 172). The account of the social contract in the earlier books makes the subjects promise not to resist the sovereign, and so it leaves the sovereign with an unimpeded natural right, but it does not give him the supreme *power* that he needs to exercise his right effectively. He needs to have the obedience of his subjects, i.e. to be assured that they will do what he commands, not merely that they will refrain from impeding him when he does what he can by himself. The doctrine of authorization, together with a covenant not to withdraw the authorization, obliges the subjects to acknowledge the sovereign's acts (or his will) as their own and so to obey his commands.

Hobbes himself may not have appreciated the full significance and importance of the new doctrine of authorization. Gauthier would probably agree with this, for he notes that the new theory should have led Hobbes to make two improvements which he in fact failed to make. (1) Hobbes presents the sovereign's right of punishing as retained from the original right of nature, but it would be more satisfactory to make it part of the right conferred by authorization. (2) In the *Leviathan* account of the kingdom of God by nature, Hobbes omits the *De Cive* doctrine of men's natural obligation to God, presumably because he perceived its inadequacy but did not know how to mend it; here again he could have invoked the kind of obligation that results from authorization.

Thomas A. Spragens, *The Politics of Motion: The World of Thomas Hobbes* (Lexington, Kentucky, and London, 1973)
The theme of this book has been described in Chapter 7. The novelty of its interpretation affects Hobbes's metaphysics more than his political theory, but Spragens does have a number of shrewd criticisms to make when he considers the views of recent interpreters of the political theory.

If scholars differ so much in their interpretations, can we hope to discover the truth? Where differing interpretations conflict with each other, not more than one can represent Hobbes's conscious intentions. But difference does not always imply incompatibility, and each of several interpretations may contain some part of the truth. Then again there may well be, indeed there are likely to be, true historical facts about the thought of Hobbes of which he himself was not aware. A historian may be able to give a true explanation of unconscious influences on a thinker which illuminate his ideas in a way that he himself did not understand. Nor is this all. Just as a thinker can fail to appreciate some significant causes of his ideas, so he can fail to appreciate some of their significant potentialities. (A clear example is Gauthier's account of further important implications that Hobbes could have drawn from his theory of authorization.) The value, even the truth, of a philosophical theory need not be confined to what its author saw in it and intended by it. So when a later commentator goes beyond purely historical explanation and takes account of fruits as well as seeds, he can well tell us things that are true. He does not tell us things that the original author intended to say (but then neither does the historian who explains the work in the light of causes and influences of which the original thinker was unaware). He does, however, tell us things that are significant for readers. He tells us what the work means, or can mean, to us, as well as what the author means to say.

I am not suggesting that incompatible accounts can all be equally true, or that we can legitimately let our imaginations run riot in reading into works of the past whatever our own background suggests to us. Hypotheses of significance can and should be restrained by canons of historical truth. They must be readings that the original author would probably have been willing to accept if they had been put to him. (For example, my own reading of Hobbes on the obligation of promises owes much to the account of promises in Hume, derived from Hobbes, and I think that Hobbes himself would have gone along with what that kindred spirit found in him.) But the history of philosophy is impoverished if it is confined to a purely historical investigation of what thinkers of the past consciously intended to say. Some of the differing interpretations of Hobbes can be definitely rejected as false. This does not mean that only one at best can be true.

INDEX

Absolute: authority 17, 20, 29, 37–8,
58–9, 71–2, 90–1; good denied 42,
47, 67; power 13, 18, 46, 98; see
also Obedience
Agreement, see Social contract
Altruism 65, 71, 95
Anarchy 30, 31, 34, 39
Animal: motion, see Motion; natural
and artificial 29–30, 83
Appearance and reality 23–6, 30, 42,
63–4
Appetite, see Desire
Aristocratic ethic 82, 89–90, 94
Aristotle 10, 17, 46, 56, 82, 85, 89;
logic 11; Poetics 44; Rhetoric
10, 44, 89
Art and nature 29
Artificial: and natural 29–30, 32, 48,
60, 77, 83, 94; bonds 33–4, 60;
justice 94; morality 48–9; obli-
gation, see Obligation
Atheism 14, 85–7
Aubrey, John 9–11, 14–15
Authority: absolute 13, 17, 20, 29,
37, 58–9; dist. power 39, 71; of
conscience 17; political 10, 17,
34–6, 57–8, 71–2, 95; sovereign
34–6, 57–8, 71–2, 84, 95
Authorization 36, 57–8, 84, 98–9
Aversion 25–7, 30–1, 41–3, 45, 67

Bacon, Francis 10–11, 95
Benevolence 15, 43–4, 65, 71, 79, 97
Bible 14, 51, 56–7, 86
Bourgeois ethic 82–3, 89–90, 93
Bramhall, Bishop John 87
Brandt, F. 88–9
Butler, Bishop Joseph 43–4, 79

Causal explanation 18–21, 24, 27–30,
35, 40, 45–6, 50, 61–2, 69, 85, 99
Causes: and definitions 19–20; and
reasons 16, 61–3; external and
internal 27, 59–60, 66
Cavendish, William, 2nd Baron (later
2nd Earl of Devonshire) 10
Charity, see Benevolence
Charles I 13, 17
Charles II 13–14
Christianity 15, 56–7, 74–5, 77, 80,
85–6, 94
Civil philosophy, see Philosophy
Claim 52–3
Clergy 13, 15
Command 32, 38, 42, 57, 75–6
Commonwealth, see State
Competition 29, 31, 49, 97
Conquest 17, 34–5, 38, 55, 59
Consciousness, see Mind
Consent 71, 95
Contract 35–7, 52–4; see also Social
contract
Counsel 76
Covenant 33–9, 53–4, 56, 58, 70–1,
76–7, 90, 92, 94, 98–100; made
from fear 55, 59; presumed 38–
9, 55, 59
Cromwell, Oliver 13
Curiosity 46, 68

De cive 13–14, 32–3, 74, 80, 94, 97–9
De Corpore 74, 81, 84, 97
De Corpore Politico 13, 33, 98: see
also Elements of Law
Deduction 11, 19–20, 95, 97
Definitions 11, 19–20, 26, 41–51, 62,
80, 97

101